Contents

SETTING OUT: A VISION OF CARRYING THE C

THE BEGINNING OF THE CROSS   **10**
ABRAHAM AND ISAAC   11
THE PASSOVER   18
ATONEMENT   24
REVERSE THE CURSE   29
WHY HAVE YOU FORSAKEN ME?   36

THE WORDS OF THE CROSS   **42**
'FATHER, FORGIVE THEM, FOR THEY KNOW NOT WHAT THEY DO.'   43
'MY GOD, MY GOD, WHY HAVE YOU FORSAKEN ME?' 'I THIRST.'   48
'FATHER, INTO YOUR HANDS I COMMIT MY SPIRIT.'   53
'WOMAN, HERE IS YOUR SON...HERE IS YOUR MOTHER.'   60
'IT IS FINISHED.'   65

THE NARRATIVE OF THE CROSS   **76**
WE ARE THE CROWD: PALM SUNDAY   77
TRANSFIGURATION AND PREDICTION   84
PASSOVER AND COMMUNION   90
GETHSEMANE AND CALLING   96
FAILURE IS NOT FINAL: PETER'S BETRAYAL   100
'THE KISS OF BETRAYAL'   107
CHALLENGING THE MYTH OF REDEMPTIVE VIOLENCE   115
JESUS BEFORE PILATE   121
'DO NOT WEEP FOR ME.' THINGS THAT KNOCK YOU SIDEWAYS   127
TORN CURTAIN AND CENTURION'S RECOGNITION   133

THE DIAMOND OF THE CROSS   **138**
TOTAL FORGIVENESS   139
AMAZING GRACE   146
DRAW NEAR TO GOD   153
REDEEMED: NO MORE CURSE OF THE LAW   159
RANSOMED   162
THE PARADOX OF THE CROSS   165
ONCE, FOR ALL   170

NO MORE SACRIFICE NEEDED   177
THE POWERS DISARMED   181
SLAVERY ENDED   188
TRUE POWER   200
GOD HAS NO SPLIT PERSONALITY   205
IT'S PERSONAL   211

THE LIFE OF THE CROSS   **217**
FREEDOM!   218
THE ABC OF GOD CONFIDENCE   227
BAPTISED INTO CHRIST   233
WE HAVE THIS MINISTRY   238
WHERE TRUE STRENGTH COMES FROM   242

THE REVELATION OF THE CROSS   **247**
THE LION AND THE LAMB   248
SOVEREIGNTY AND SACRIFICE   253

Setting Out: A Vision of Carrying The Cross
Luke 9:23-24
Guy Donegan-Cross. 7th January 2018

Our vision is of being a family of servants on mission is beautiful, but in some ways it is not attractive.

Being a family with the same Father is a wonderful thing. But if we are really going to belong together – to people we don't choose, maybe don't click with, because of Jesus, that will cost us. It will demand sacrifice.

And being servants like Christ is again a wonderful calling. As Martin Luther King said, 'Anyone can be great, because anyone can serve.' But washing people's feet, giving up your time for others, persevering when things aren't going well, not being thanked for menial tasks, because of Jesus, that will cost you. Church will not be what you get out of it, but what you contribute. It will demand sacrifice.

And being on mission is to embrace a sense of purpose and calling. But it will shake us out of our comfort zones. We are the light of the world? Really? We have to make disciples? That will cost you. It will demand sacrifice.

Why are we focusing on the cross, and Luke 9? Because until we know deep in our souls what the cross means, we won't live for Christ, for each other, or for the world. The more we see the cross, the more we will be willing to sacrifice, to die to our own needs, comfort, idols, and to live lives for Him.

Missionaries in the nineteenth century, before they went overseas, would pack their belongings in a coffin instead of a trunk so they would have something to be buried in. They never expected to return. Imagine saying goodbye to your family, your

3

friends to follow Jesus' call. Imagine them watching that coffin disappear round the corner.

The truth is, as a Christian, you are already dead. You have already entered eternal life, you have left behind the securities of creature comforts, your own priorities...Paul said, 'I have been crucified with Christ and I no longer live, but Christ lives in me.' And he said to the Colossians, 'For you died, and your life is now hidden with Christ in God.' And to the Corinthians, 'And as for us, why do we endanger ourselves every hour? I die every day -- I mean that, brothers...'

When Jesus told his disciples to take up their cross every day, he was painting a picture. A picture of people who would live their lives as if they were on the path he was travelling. Dead people walking.

Am I selling it to you? It's no wonder people fell away from him. It's no wonder people give up the faith sometimes.

But the amazing thing is that disciples seemed to think this was a good idea. That losing their lives in order to find them was worth everything. It was like they had seen something, experienced something that created an epiphany. A moment of realisation which made carrying a cross for Jesus their privilege. What was going on?

What I'd like to be able to do today is convince myself, and you, that denying myself, taking up my cross daily, losing my self is the best thing that could possibly happen to me. That every other path of life is pale by comparison. That we could go out willing to make the sacrifices of being family, being servants on mission, with our coffins packed and ready to go! And here is why:

Firstly, because the point is not about denying yourself. Denying yourself as an end in itself is actually a tedious and pointless idea. Who really likes dieting? It robs life of joy. Simply telling people to deny themselves, as some spirituality does, is the opposite of what Jesus is talking about here. A lot of damage has been done in the history of the world, and sadly in the story of our brothers and sisters, by people being brought up to believe that what God wants is for them to effectively hate their bodies, be ashamed of themselves, and be suspicious of joy. 'Whoever wants to be my disciple must deny themselves and take up their cross daily and follow me.' If we just put a full stop after 'deny yourself', we miss the point. After all he goes on to talk about the aim being to find yourself. The point is, Jesus is calling you to follow Him. It's not about punishing yourself, it's about embracing Him. It's not about being a worm, it's about making space for him to be at the centre. Making space to follow. Please stop just denying yourself! After all, Jesus then says, 'whoever loses their life for my sake, will find it.' And that means, forever. If you make space for Him at the centre, He says, you will gain everything – real, true, eternal life. The real you as He sees you. If that's the prize, get rid of everything that you put in your own way, and follow Him.

Here's another marvellous truth. If you know you have already died, what or who can harm you? What can you lose any more? Jesus once said, 'Don't be afraid of those who can kill the body, but can't kill the soul.' If you insult me, why should I care because I have already died? I am carrying my cross. There is nothing your insult can do to me. If I am poor, what does it matter? I am already walking the path to eternal life. We all have worries, anxieties, challenges in life. But if you see them as things that belong to a life you have left, because you are walking in a different life, then what significance can those things have any more? What is there really to be afraid of? It's the path to freedom, isn't it? The more we know we have already died, the less we fear our physical death.

Taking up your cross and following Jesus is as well the way to be freed from our illusions about what really matters in life. Jesus' call is to put everything else second compared to following Him. Die to your possessions. Die to your own comfort. Die to your reputation. Die to your need for recognition. And put Him first. And here is the freedom you gain. You realise that all those things you might live for, that you cling to – your career, your success, your materialism – they cannot bring life anyway. What is there in those things that will last? What is there in those things that will give you a stable sense of who you are? They will all disappear. The idea that you will find meaning and fulfilment in things that will not last is an illusion. Instead, Jesus' words are a massive reality check. Follow me, because I am the only way to life.

God's desire is that we gain our true selves. Forever. I have a friend who once had a tattoo on her arm of the Chinese character for death. It said on the outside a lot about how she felt on the inside. But she had an epiphany, a realisation. She not only understood it, she experienced it. And her heart began to be melted into a new shape. And instead she now has covered that Chinese character with a different tattoo. That of the cross. And the words, 'If God is for us, who can be against us.' The point is, that seeing the cross shifted her identity. It shifted not only what she does, but who she is. You could say she is gaining her life, for Jesus' sake.

There's a common myth that we have it in ourselves to find ourselves. If we travel enough, get enough experiences, read enough or whatever we will find ourselves. At the centre of who we are there is a 'Me' waiting to be discovered. But the truth is we are more like onions, and if we continue peeling the layers away, we eventually discover that we cannot find out who we are by ourselves. Instead who we are is revealed by what we are committed to, by what we serve. If you serve money, that shapes who you are. Whatever we live for and die for shapes who we are. Who you are is a byproduct of what you serve, who you follow. And Jesus says, 'If you lose yourself in serving me you will find out who you really are.'

There are lots of good reasons why dying to yourself, taking up your cross, and living self-sacrificially is great for you and I. In fact, by being committed to a family of Christians, by serving, and by following God's mission, you and I can also be living sacrifices who show people a bit what Jesus' love looks like. We put flesh and blood on the way of the cross.

But none of these come close to the real reason, or the real motive. None of these reasons make sense of the Christians down the ages who have packed their coffins early, pursued God's calling profoundly, and made Jesus Lord.

The real reason is because they love Jesus. They see His love, the one who was handed over to torture, death and degradation, and they want to follow. They are blinded by His grace.

A man was on a train leaving London. Sitting across from him were two men in their late thirties. About ten minutes out if the station, one of the men had an epileptic seizure. His eyes rolled back and his body trembled. The man rolled off the seat onto the floor and shook uncontrollably. It was a shocking thing to see. His friend lifted the stricken man up and put him back on the seat, took off his overcoat, and put it around him as a blanket. He rolled up a newspaper and put it in his mouth, lest the man bite his tongue. Then with great compassion, he lovingly blotted the beads of perspiration on the epileptic man's forehead. After a few minutes, the seizure ended with the same abruptness with which it began, and the stricken man dropped into a deep sleep.

The friend apologised, 'You'll have to forgive us. He doesn't have these seizures very often, but we never know when they are going to strike him.' 'We were at war together,' he continued. 'We were both wounded. I lost a leg.' Pointing to his right leg he said, 'This is an artificial leg. I've learned to walk on it very well. My friend here had half his chest blown away by a hand grenade.

There was shrapnel all through his chest, and every time he moved he experienced great pain. There was no hope of rescue.

Somehow my friend picked himself up. He screamed in pain with every move he made, but somehow he stood to his feet. Then he reached down and grabbed hold of my shirt and started to pull me through the jungle. I tried to tell him to give up on me. I pleaded with him to save himself if he could, and I kept telling him there was no way he was going to get us both out of the jungle. I'll never forget him saying. 'Jack, if you die in this jungle, I'm going to die here with you.' I don't know how he did it, but step by step, scream by scream, he pulled me out of that mess. He saved my life!'

'A year ago I found out that he had this condition and that somebody had to be with him all the time. So I closed down my house, sold my car and came over here to take care of him. That's out story. I hope you understand.' The man responded by saying, 'Don't apologise. I'm a preacher. Whenever I come upon a good story, I'm thrilled. And this is one of the best stories I've heard in a long, long time.' The man replied, 'Hey! Don't be impressed. You see, after what he did for me, there isn't anything I wouldn't do for him.'

Only by seeing the cross more and more will we want to say, 'I have been crucified with Christ and I no longer live, but Christ lives in me. The life I now live in the body, I live by faith in the Son of God, who loved me and gave himself for me.' Only knowing and seeing this grace, this love, this beauty will make us want to follow this vision.

There are not regular Christians, or churchgoers, and then disciples. There are only disciples. If you want to be a disciple this is the path. When you walk out of here today, you are invited to take up and carry a cross. To be a dead person walking. Self-sacrificial enough to embrace a new family. Following Jesus enough to serve. To be on mission. You have already packed, you have already begun your resurrected life. You know whose you are. And then, tomorrow, morning to pick it up again. Until the day you lay it down at Jesus' feet.

The Beginning of The Cross

Abraham and Isaac
The Passover
Atonement
Reverse the Curse
Why have you forsaken me?

The Beginning of The Cross

Abraham and Isaac

Genesis 22:1-19, Matthew 7:21-23
Dan Watts. 14th January 2018

A man was walking along a narrow path, not paying much attention to where he was going. Suddenly he slipped over the edge of a cliff. As he fell, he grabbed a branch growing from the side of the cliff. Realising that he couldn't hang on for long, he called for help.

Man: Is anybody up there?
Voice: Yes, I'm here!
Man: Who's that?
Voice: The Lord.
Man: Lord, help me!
Voice: Do you trust me?
Man: I trust you completely, Lord.
Voice: Good. Let go of the branch.
Man: What???
Voice: I said, let go of the branch.
Man: [After a long pause] Is anybody else up there?

Like this dangling cliffhanger, have you ever afraid that God might ask too much of you?

Consider for a moment what would be too much? Our daily lives are built around people and things we enjoy: a spouse, children, friends, a job, a hobby, possessions, and future plans. In Genesis 22 we come to one of the greatest chapters in the entire Bible. It is a story of promise, obedience, salvation and provision. It is a story of crisis. It brings in to sharp focus the crisis of obedience that we all face. Who will you obey? Who will be the Lord of your life? It is a story about the way God keeps his promise from generation to generation in the lives of ordinary people.

God chose Abraham to be the means through which he would rebuild a relationship with his creation. God makes a promise to Abram to make his name great, to make him into a great nation, to bless him in order that his family and nation might be a blessing to the whole world. So God makes a covenant promise and seals it in blood. Abraham's identity is rooted in that of his covenant partner Yahweh. The two become one and so The Lord promises to be Abram's provided and protector and Abraham will live in obedience to the Lord.

Remember that this chapter started with the words 'God tested Abraham'. It was a test to prove his love, obedience and devotion to God. Faith is like a muscle: it grows stronger with frequent use. It is perhaps encouraging to remember that this test is not the first test Abraham faced. He had failed many of the earlier tests (maybe there is even hope for you and I). Remember when God first called Abram to leave his Father's household and his native country, he only partially obeyed, as he took his Father on the journey too. He went as far as Haran, and only after his father's death and the subsequent call of God, did Abram fully obey. When he finally got to Canaan, there was a famine. Without seeking God, Abram went down to Egypt, and there he failed by passing off Sarah as his sister. Later in the story, when God delayed fulfilling the promise of a son, Abram failed by having relations with Hagar, which resulted in the birth of Ishmael.

Abraham really only desired one thing: a son, an heir. So that he will have descendants as numerous as the stars of the sky. There is absolutely nothing more precious to Abraham than his son. Indeed, to give up his son would be to give up himself.

As we read through this account, we see that it says nothing about Abraham's emotional reaction to this request of God's. I think the reason is that it was quite unnecessary to say anything. We instinctively know what this must have meant to Abraham. I think we can safely assume, that as a loving father, he must have been very troubled in his heart, and must have shed tears in great anguish. He must have been bemused, angry, fearful all at the same time.

How could God be asking this of him? And yet, the voice is unmistakable; he has heard this voice many times. You can almost imagine the conversation - This is Isaac; this is the son of promise, this is the one you yourself gave me. Why are you asking me to put him to death like this? Is that really you speaking Lord? These must have been some of the questions that arose in his heart. What a sleepless, troubled night of torture and heartbreak this man went through.

Now, notice that, when morning comes, Abraham's obedience is prompt and complete. Though his heart is torn he still obeys God. He has passed the test. Throughout his life he has been learning to submit to his covenant partner, the one who has promised to both provide and protect. Is this not the lifetime journey of all who are called to discipleship – 'take up your cross and follow me'? We are so inclined to excuse ourselves from hard, uncomfortable things and to rationalise our way out of difficult situations, relieving the pressure and avoiding certain unpleasant situations. We don't like disturbing questions, and unsettling challenges. We don't like sacrifice; we don't like to think someone else might know better than me; we don't like someone else being in control. When it comes right down to it, we don't like to take hold of ourselves, and say, 'I am going to obey God!'

Abraham and Isaac take wood, fire and a knife and head up the mountain to worship Yahweh and offer a burnt sacrifice. Again the record is silent about the emotional reaction of Abraham here, but we have only to put ourselves in his place to sense what he felt, how his heart was torn, how he avoids telling Isaac the fearful truth until the very last possible moment, how he perhaps trembles within when Isaac asks the question, 'Where is the lamb?' We know there is no real answer to Isaac's question until we run through intervening centuries and listen in the New Testament to John the Baptist standing before the people of Israel saying, 'Behold, the Lamb of God who takes away the sin of the world.'

Isaac is bound and laid on the wooden altar. Where did this grief stricken father find the strength to be obedient? The answer is found here in one brief phrase in Verse 5, 'Then Abraham said to his servants, "Stay here with the donkey while I and the boy go over there. We will worship and then we will come back to you."' We will both be coming back again. Abraham is not trying to deceive these men, but somewhere in the quiet meditations of that awful night when this word first came to him, there came the consciousness that God could do something to raise this boy from the dead and Abraham believed in resurrection. That is where he found the peace to follow God's command. In the struggles of that night, he began to reason and to reckon on God,

He must have thought something like this: 'God is my covenant partner. God has given me promises and I have lived with God long enough to know that when God gives a promise, he carries it through. God has said that in my son, Isaac, all the nations of the earth shall be blessed. Isaac is necessary to the fulfilment of the promise. It can't be any other way; he has said this boy is the one who is going to be the fulfilment of the promise. Well, then, if God has asked me now to offer him up as a sacrifice, there is only one explanation. God intends to raise him from the dead.'

Abraham had no experience or record of anyone having risen from the dead. He knew nothing of Easter, or of Lazarus, or the miracles in the Gospel accounts. Yet so firm is his faith in the character of God that he comes to a realisation of the resurrection. This is confirmed in Hebrews 11:19 'By faith Abraham ... offered up Isaac,' 'Abraham reasoned that God could raise the dead...' And so, to this father, as he is traveling on the way to Mt Moriah, Isaac has been as good as dead in his eyes for three days. Abraham risked everything he owned and loved upon the character of God, his covenant partner, and found him to be a God of resurrection, a God of provision and protection.

God commanded Abraham to travel about 50 miles to sacrifice Isaac at *just* this location on Mt Moriah, without ever offering an explanation. It is as if God expected something special to happen there later?

There is no clearer picture of the Cross and the sacrifice the Father made for us in Christ than Genesis chapter 22. It is a wonderful foreshadowing of the work of Christ on the cross. It seems to me that no one watching old Abraham binding his dear son to the altar and his heart breaking within him can miss the parallel with God sending his own Son to Calvary's mountain centuries later.

Notice the powerful parallels between Isaac and Christ.
- Both fulfilled promises:
  Isaac was the long-promised son to Abraham (Genesis 12:3)
  Jesus was the long-promised Messiah (Genesis 3:15; 13:3)

- Both were the only sons of their father:
  God said that Isaac was 'Your son, your only son, whom you live...' to Abraham (Genesis 22:2)
  God said, 'This is my beloved son in whom I am well pleased!' (Matthew 3:16-17)

- Both were loved by their fathers (Genesis 22:2; Matthew 3:16-17).

- Both had a 3-day experience
  Isaac had a 3-day hike to Mt Moriah
  Jesus had 3 days from the cross to the grave to the resurrection

- Both accompanied by 2 men:
  Isaac by two servants (Genesis 22:3)
  Jesus by two thieves (Matthew 27:38)

- Both carried their own wood:
  Isaac carried the wood for his own sacrifice (Genesis 22:6)
  Jesus carried the crossbeam of his cross (John 19:17)

- Both submitted to their father:
  Isaac willingly lay down, submitting to his father (Genesis 22:9)
  Jesus submitted to his Father's plan and will (Luke 22:42)

The most important truth in relation to the Christian journey of discipleship is that Jesus Christ is Lord. Our Saviour's great objective in all His redemptive work was 'that He might be Lord' in the life of every believer (see Philippians 2:5-11). Whether we recognise it or not, He is Lord. In recognition of His work in redemption, God has constituted His Son 'both Lord and Christ'. He is King of Kings and Lord of Lords. Our Lord Jesus Christ has no equal and no rival. He has no superior; there is none before, beside or beyond Him: 'For this very reason, Christ died and returned to life so that he might be the Lord of both the dead and the living' Romans 14:9.

I wonder if too often we focus on Jesus as Saviour, we relate to him as the one that loves and saves us, we receive and experience his grace and forgiveness perhaps at the expense of recognising Jesus' sovereignty, of His right to rule. The One whom we call Saviour is also our Lord. Accepting Him as Saviour implies submitting to Him as Sovereign. The One whom we receive as our Saviour is also the LORD; the One who sits on the throne; the One who is to be obeyed. It is great to rejoice in Him as our Saviour, but unless we have recognised that He is the Lord Jesus Christ, and have submitted to His lordship, we have not entered into the full meaning of what it is to be a disciple. What is He to you, now? Jesus or the Lord Jesus.

Karen Watson (an American Baptist Missionary) was killed in Iraq in 2004. She wrote a letter to pastor to be opened at her death: 'You should only be opening this letter in the event of my death. When God calls there are no regrets. I tried to share my heart with you as much as possible, my heart for the Nations. I wasn't called to a place. I was called to Him. To obey was my objective, to suffer was expected. His glory was my reward. His glory is my reward.' She closed by saying; 'Care more than some think is wise. Risk more than some think is safe. Dream more than some think is practical. Expect more than some think is possible. I was called not to comfort or success but to obedience.'

And that is His call to us all! The life of a disciple is a call to live a life of obedience to Jesus as Lord.

What is the 'Isaac' in your life? What idol are you worshiping? What has taken the rightful place of the Lord Jesus?

What do we need to let go of, so that Jesus Can be Lord of ALL.

The Beginning of The Cross

The Passover

Exodus 12:1-28
Dave Mumford. 21st January 2018

John the Baptist was an interesting character. A wild and holy
prophet whose whole mission in life was to prepare the way for
the LORD Jesus. In fact, John was prophesied in the Old
Testament as one who would cry out in the wilderness and
introduce Jesus to the world. And when his big moment came to
announce Christ onto the world stage, what did John say?

'Behold the Lamb of God who takes away the sin of the world.'
(John 1:29)

Think of all the ways John could have described Jesus. He could
have said 'Behold the Son of God', 'Behold the Son of
Righteousness', 'Behold the Light of the World,' 'Behold the Lord
of Israel', 'Behold the great I AM', 'Behold the Maker of heaven
and earth He could have chosen any of those, but here's what
John thought we needed to know first: 'Behold the Lamb of God.'
Behold the Sacrifice. Behold God's Bleeding Victim. This is how
He introduced Jesus.

So then if we want to understand and know – if we want to learn
what it means to 'Behold Jesus', we must understand Him as the
Lamb. And the only way we can understand this is through the
lens of the Passover – in Exodus 12.

This morning we're going to quickly get a handle on: The details
of Passover, then we're going to see how Passover fits into the
whole of the Bible, then we're going to draw out some
implications.

So first the details...
Perhaps the first thing to say about Passover is, Passover was a plague! The heading for chapter 11 gives the other name for the Passover, it was 'the plague on the firstborn.'

There have been nine plagues prior to this one – nine signs to Pharaoh that the LORD is not to be reckoned with and Pharaoh really should let His people go. Each time Pharaoh refuses and each time his heart gets harder and therefore the plagues get deadlier and deadlier as time goes on until finally, Exodus 11:4 Moses explains that the firstborn son in every family in Egypt will die – including Pharaoh's. He says 'then you will know that the LORD makes a distinction between Egypt and Israel.'

What's the distinction that the LORD is going to make? Is He just going to avoid the Israelite suburbs and only visit the Egyptians?

No, He's going to pass through the whole country. The distinction will be – some will take shelter under the blood of a lamb and the LORD will pass over them, the rest will be judged. Well then, how do you take shelter? Chapter 12, verse 3 – on the 10th day of the 1st month, take a lamb into your household. It has to be a lamb – it doesn't work if they all sacrificed a budgie. We used to have a pet rabbit called Charlie Muffin – guess who named him? He used hop around our house and whenever we had visitors he would try and get them to leave by leaving droppings all around their feet. I asked the Lord many times, if he required me to make a sacrifice – I was willing!

But in this –Only a lamb will do. Verse 5, the lamb has to be male – it's going to stand in for the firstborn son, so it's 'like for like'. And it has to be without defect – not some cheap old thing, a precious lamb without spot.

Verse 3 says, adopt it into family life – Floppy will become a pet for the next 4 days – one of the family. But on the 14th day of the month at twilight I'm afraid Floppy gets it in the neck. Then (v22) using a bit of hyssop plant as a paintbrush, paint the blood on the outside of your doorframes. Then go inside and don't come out again till morning – you're only safe as you shelter under the blood of the lamb. Once inside (verses 8-11), roast the lamb with bitter herbs and eat it with unleavened bread. Eat it fast, eat it standing, eat it ready to leave the country because this is the last night you'll ever be in Egypt.

Verse 23 – at midnight when the LORD goes through the land, He will pass over every house which shelters under the blood of the lamb. But, v29, for the Egyptians who did not heed the LORD's warnings He strikes down the firstborn of every household. And after this plague, Pharaoh finally lets the Israelites go and forevermore the Israelites would commemorate Passover as their liberation from Egypt.

Those are the details of Passover.
But let me give some context in the bible.

Let's rewind 500 years – to the story of Abraham and Isaac which you heard about last week. The LORD halts the sacrifice of Isaac and provides an alternative – in this case a ram.
The ram dies instead of Isaac. But from that day onwards that mountain was called 'The LORD WILL provide.'

What will the LORD provide? The Lamb. The LORD will provide the Lamb on that mountain in the region of Jerusalem. He will be the true beloved Son. The true sacrifice of atonement. And He will carry the wood up that very hill to die for the sins of the world.

Fast forward 800 years and we fly over a thousand references to lambs and sacrifices and blood of a helpless victim but we come to Isaiah chapter 53. He prophesies the work of the Messiah saying: 'He was led like a lamb to the slaughter, and as a sheep before her shearers is silent, so He did not open His mouth.' (Isaiah 53:7)

Isaiah goes onto to say 5 He was pierced for our transgressions, He was crushed for our iniquities; the punishment that brought us peace was upon Him, and by His wounds we are healed. 6We all, like sheep, have gone astray, each of us has turned to his own way; and the LORD has laid on Him the iniquity of us all.

Isaiah knew that the coming Christ – He would be the Lamb of God, and He would die in our place to bring us shelter, healing, forgiveness and peace.

Fast forward another 700 years and Jesus is entering Jerusalem on a donkey. It's the tenth day of the first month – and as all of Israel are bringing their Passover lambs into their houses, Jesus enters into the house of God. And on the 14th day of the 1st month, while everyone else is holding their Passover meals, Jesus is hosting His last supper. Except he appears to be doing it all wrong. He's meant to be carving the lamb and passing it around. But there is no lamb on the menu – there's just some bread and some wine. Jesus, the lamb of God then takes bread and wine into His hands and says 'Remember My body broken for you. My blood shed for you.'

And then on the cross Jesus dies that bloody Passover death – a Lamb to the slaughter.

No wonder the Apostle Paul says, 1 Corinthians 5:7 – 'Christ our Passover Lamb has been sacrificed.'

Peter writes 1 Peter 1:19 – 'You were redeemed with the precious blood of Christ, a Lamb without blemish or defect.'

And when the Apostle John wrote Revelation he calls Jesus 'the Lamb' 28 times.

So what we see here in Exodus, it's not just an account of one remarkable night in ancient history. Passover reveals the most fundamental truths about our LORD Jesus and the theme and understanding of Christ as the Passover lamb is webbed together throughout scripture. That's awesome isn't it. I mean we are privileged to have this today as one narrative.

3 ways that we can take all of this and apply to our own lives from all of this today:

1. It'll transform the way you view other people.

Even a Hebrew is no better than an Egyptian if you buy this understanding of a Passover God – the God of the cross. Do you realise that you're no better than everyone else? It totally transforms your view of others. The truth is the cross is Jesus dying for people that didn't believe in him. It makes you realise that you're no better than the people you dislike – only in him are you loved.

2. It'll transform your view of Glory and achievement.

In our culture – Glory and achievement is acquiring – attaining. The cross says Glory is servicing – it's giving, giving away. [Story of meeting Ash at The Ark] who said 'Social Action' – I find 'glory' in it..

3. It'll transform your view of suffering

The most undeserved suffering in the history of the world changed everything. The most apparently senseless suffering – worked out to the most good. That should transform our view of our own suffering.

If I really 'Beheld' the lamb of God – my attitude would be different towards others, attitude towards my life and achievement would be different, towards my own suffering would be different. But it's important to Eat the lamb with others. Christianity is an eternal Passover meal – so eat with others who have had the same experience and you say.... why has this happened? Why have I been saved? And you behold the lamb of God together until it sinks in and you're transformed.

Do you know, if you stopped an Israelite in the desert of Sinai and you asked them – what are you guys – what are you doing? You know what they would have said? They would have said 'I was an alien in a foreign land, under the penalty of death, but I took shelter under the blood of the lamb and even though morally, racially, ethically I could not save myself – I was saved and now, I've been brought out – and God is in our midst and even though looking around life isn't perfect – I mean I'm in a desert, but I know that He's taking me to the promised land and that is exactly what our story should be because everything in the history of the world – everything through the bible – it all climaxed on the day when Jesus became the lamb of God who takes away the sins of the world.

Prayer
Help understand why Jesus died. Help us to change our view towards others. Help us change our view of Glory, Help us change our view of suffering and walk together in community, breaking bread, drinking wine and beholding you as the lamb of God knowing that it will transform us from the inside out – we ask of this we pray today. Amen.

The Beginning of The Cross

Atonement

Leviticus 16:2-10, 29-34, Matthew 27:50-51
James Handley. 28th January 2018

I'm guessing that for most of us here, Leviticus isn't one of our favourite books of the bible! It's full of rules and regulations, many of which can seem bizarre, irrelevant or – at times – offensive to us. But I think we shouldn't dismiss Leviticus too quickly, because it has a lot to teach us about God, about ourselves, and about Jesus himself – after all, Leviticus was a core text of his scriptures.

Today's reading definitely falls into the category of the bizarre or even offensive. Animals are being slaughtered, special clothes are worn, there's ritual washing. And we only had about half the passage read to us! It feels a very long way removed from Harrogate in 2018.

I think the key to understanding what is going on here, and what it has to do with the cross, lies in the very first verse we heard: 'Aaron can't come in [to the Most Holy Place] whenever he pleases... or else he will die'. (Leviticus 16:2) You see, God had a bit of a problem. On the one hand, He wanted to live among His people. On the other hand He is so holy, so pure, that anyone who has any impurity, any sin, cannot survive in his presence. Just as staring directly at the sun for more than a few seconds can cause permanent damage to our eyes, our mortal souls and bodies cannot withstand God. I think we sometimes forgot about how awesome (in the technical sense) God is. About how pure, how holy, how much like a consuming fire.

The answer to this problem in Old Testament times was twofold. Firstly, God choose to be present in a very specific way, where he could be present but still separate. Secondly, God provided a way for His people generally, and the High Priest specifically, to be able to be reconciled with Him.

The way that God was present but separate was in the tabernacle, essentially a large tent. This would be packed up and carried with the Israelites whenever they were on the move, and then put up again whenever they made camp. You can read all about it in Exodus 26. It consisted of a large enclosed outer courtyard, and at one end of this courtyard was a tent, called the Holy Place. Inside the Holy Place was a curtained off area called the Most Holy Place. And it was in this Most Holy Place that God dwelt. And as the 'holiness' increased as you went inwards, so did the rules about who could enter into that part. So only Jews could enter the courtyard, only the priests could enter the Holy Place, and only the High Priest could enter the Most Holy Place, and even then only once a year, on the Day of Atonement. This separation meant that God could be there, living among the people, but apart from that so that they wouldn't be destroyed by his holiness.

But being present but separated wasn't enough – God still wanted relationship with His people, which is where Atonement comes in. Actually, a much better pronunciation is 'at-one-ment'; The word itself is a 16th Century English translation of the Hebrew word 'Kipur' - the Hebrew name for this festival being 'Yom Kipur'. 'Kipur' means 'covering over' (in the sense of 'covering the cost of the repairs', rather than hiding out of view), or reconciliation, or becoming 'at one'. Hence what is going on in Kipur is that we are becoming 'at-one' with God, or you might say that it's an 'at-one-ment'.

So, on the Day of 'At-one-ment,' the High Priest would undertake this elaborate ritual, to make offerings first of all on behalf of himself, and then for the whole of the Israeli people, so that he and they could be 'at one' with God, and the High Priest could enter into God's presence. When I read all the elaborate preparations, and the care that is taken, with washing and putting on special clothes, it reminds me a bit of people getting into Hazmat suits – like when there was the Ebola outbreak. A great deal of care must be taken to ensure the suit is undamaged, that all the gaps have been taped up, that the masks fit properly. There's almost a ritualistic element to it. So much care has to be taken, because it is an extremely serious, dangerous and contagious scenario. In that sense, it is quite like sin, which is also extremely serious, dangerous and contagious. It's also quite clear that the suit is for the protection of the person wearing it, not for the benefit of the patient. And in that sense this is also like sin. It's not that God needs shielding from us, or is offended by us and or sin – but that we would be utterly destroyed by his purity and holiness if we were exposed to it in our sinful state. Before he could come before God, Aaron needed these elaborate precautions for his own sake.

So, we have these two 'solutions' to the problem of sin – the separation of the people from God, and this ceremony of 'at-one-ment'. But why is sin such a problem anyway? And why does there have to be a sacrifice to deal with it? These are big questions which we will return to again over the course of this year, but we can get some insight into why sin is taken so seriously from the perspective of Leviticus 16.

Firstly, sin separates us from God. It has to, because otherwise we would be utterly consumed. Sin is anything which is contrary to God's nature and has also been described as acts of rebellion against God. This is, by definition, a barrier, a break in relationship.

Secondly, sin is contagious. It spreads throughout the community like any other sickness would. A closely related term used in the Bible is 'uncleanliness', which is also infectious. It pollutes us and our world. It corrupts individuals and society. The rules and regulations I mentioned at the start are to do with trying to keep this corruption in check, and how to deal with it when it happens.

Thirdly, and in any ways this is the heart of 'Kipur', it has a cost to making it right. The cost of sin must be covered, so that we can be at-one with God again.

I found Tim Keller's book 'The Reason for God' really helpful in understanding what the cost of sin means. I've adapted his analogy slightly, so bear with me – but suppose I was to drop a glass, and it breaks. There is now a cost associated with this making this right. Firstly, someone has to sweep up all the bits of glass, to tidy up the mess. Secondly, a new glass has to be purchased to replace the one that has broken. Anyone can pay this cost – it might be me, or Guy, or the cleaners; but unless someone does, it remains a dangerous mess, and we have one less glass. The cost is inherent and unavoidable. I may have deliberately broken it, I may have accidentally knocked it over, I may not even be aware that I broke it. None of this changes the fact there is a cost to making it right. And so, sin is a bit like dropping of a glass – there is an inherent and unavoidable cost which must be paid to put it right, to put things back to how they were before. Paul writes in Romans 6, 'the wages of sin are death', and the unavoidable and inherent cost of sin is death. Somehow – and the Bible is not completely clear on the how – the blood of these animals can serve the purpose of paying this price, of putting things right again. That the sacrifice of the animal is in a way spiritually analogous to sweeping up bits of glass....

...at least until the next time a glass is dropped. And that's the nub. The Day of Atonement didn't actually work. Each and every year the High Priest had to do it all over again because he and Israel kept on sinning. The cost of putting it right kept coming back. So, each year more animals, more ritual, to try and deal with this sickness.

Leviticus 16 shows us the seriousness of sin, and of our separation from God. It shows that we can be made right with God – to be at one with Him, but there is a cost.

But it does make you wonder - what might it take to deal with it once and for all?

Maybe there could be a new, permanent High Priest? A High Priest so radical that he would, of his own free will, sacrifice himself instead of animals. That this High Priest would be so pure and powerful and perfect, that his sacrifice would affect not only a covering but a complete reversal of sin? Someone who so comprehensively covers the cost of sin, that the curtain around the Most Holy Place is torn in two, so that all can become at-one with God, for all time. That no longer would we need elaborate precautions to come into the presence of God. Someone who so comprehensively covers the cost of sin that the glass no longer even breaks when it is dropped? That instead of the *glass* shattering, the one who has taken its place shatters. That instead of the glass being broken, the body of the one who has taken its place is broken. That as he foresaw his body being broken, his blood poured out, he might say 'this is my body, given for you', and 'this is my blood, shed for you'.

Can we imagine such a person?

The Beginning of The Cross

Reverse the Curse

Deuteronomy 21:22-23, Numbers 21:5-9
Guy Donegan-Cross. 4th February 2018

This might sound like a bit of an obvious question but do you think the world is the way it's meant to be? I mean, when you consider all that's wrong with it does it strike you as something *normal*? Something *that should be expected*? Something that's *just the way it is*? Children being barrel bombed? Human beings being trafficked? The oceans being filled with trash? Nations making war? Is that *normality*? Or is it distortion to you?

And here's another question: do you think human beings are all that we are meant to be? Is it *normal* that we should be selfish? That we should fall out? We should make war? That millions should be in poverty? Is that *just the way it should be* to you, or is it a sign of something drastically wrong?

I guess what I'm trying to get at is, 'Are we, am I, and is the world the best it's meant to be, or a distortion of what it's called to be?'

We might not be surprised to learn that Scripture teaches from the word go that things are not as they should be. In fact, it's not just that things have slipped a bit, but that they have become twisted, pulled apart, distorted and warped. We live in a world that is a gift, but also a battleground.

This is where the language of *curse* comes from. We think of curses as something to do with witches, angry gods, or occult behaviour. But in the Scripture anything that has been twisted from what it should be is under a curse.

Curse language is the Bible's way of signalling to us just how far things have fallen. Things have been twisted from where they should be. One of the reasons I am a Christian is because of the way that Scripture does not flinch from reality.

The Old Testament in particular paints a picture of a world that could have been, and yet a world that has been so warped by evil and alienation.

In Genesis human beings are alienated from God by their initial choices. They experience the curse of being uprooted from the source of love and life. To be truly cursed - twisted away from who you are made to be - is to be alienated from the love of God. In Matthew Jesus paints a picture where those who reject God are cursed - exiled from the presence and glory of God. Do you see evidence of that curse today? People who live as if God doesn't matter, or people who live believing that they don't matter to Him?

And they become alienated from each other - no longer living in harmony but constantly needing to seek reconciliation. Is that an accurate description of us? Into the world comes crime and punishment. In those early days crimes are punishable by death, by people being hung on poles. God declares this a curse – a heart-breaking aberration, a distortion, twisting of all that He intended. Is this a primitive picture, or a contemporary one?

The picture Genesis gives us is that the world itself has become twisted from what it should be. God describes how because of the fall even the ground will become cursed, producing thorns and thistles. And in a passage from Deuteronomy we see a description of the *land* being desecrated by the actions of human beings. So the land is cursed - creation blighted. Do you see any evidence of this today? Any evidence that things aren't as they should be? Plastic in the oceans? Melting ice caps? Oil spills? Water shortages?

Jesus prays, 'Deliver us from evil.' There is a diagnosis of spiritual curse throughout the Bible. God creates heavenly beings and earthly beings and yet even the heavenly beings rebel. The snake becomes an emblem of spiritual rebellion. The opposite of God. The twisting of the angelic, the holy, the secret, into lies, deceit and destruction. Right from the beginning there is an acknowledgement of evil which is bigger than us. Principalities and powers. Do you sense the curse of this battle? Or is it just that the world has slipped a bit?

CS Lewis portrays the curse in 'The Lion, the Witch and the Wardrobe' as a 'winter' that lies over Narnia. A winter caused by a white witch who needs to be defeated. A winter that is waiting to end.

And it's worth mentioning to that this winter can be a winter of the spirit. Later on in the Bible Paul talks about those who are under 'the curse of the law.' What does he mean? I think he is actually referring to religious people here - but people who think that loving God is simply about trying to satisfy his demands. People who live under the nervous anxiety of never being good enough. And here even God has become twisted. Because the one who is in fact perfect love has become one who causes guilt and fear. The 'curse of the law' is that even though God has made us for freedom we experience him as condemnation.

You may think I'm labouring the point, but it's easy for us to trivialise the depth and nature of our predicament, or to misunderstand the language of curse in the Bible. It's hard to read in the Old Testament that God curses people, or allows them to experience the curse. I just have a couple of things here by way of a footnote. One is that we have got to get away from the idea that God is a vindictive God who loves to curse. This language is just describing the reality of the way the world is when it turns away from him. The second thing to say is that if we're honest God is sometimes portrayed in the Old Testament in ways that don't seem loving. Recently I've been coming to believe that this is actually evidence of how far God will stoop to us. God is not vindictive, cursing, or random. But He will allow us to portray Him and even understand Him as less than He is if the prize is that He can stay close to us. When we read in the Old Testament God speaking and acting in ways that don't look like Jesus we have to believe that it's evidence not of His true character, but of His loving willingness to accommodate himself at the loss of His own reputation. It's a bit like a parent allowing his children to think of him as a criminal if the prize is that He is able to protect their lives.

So what we see in the Old Testament is an acknowledgement of a curse -one that has become more profoundly obvious as history continues. And a curse that I believe if we're honest with ourselves we probably see evidence of day by day, both outside and within.

The Bible is unflinching in its diagnosis-but it's also beautiful in its cure. And in the Old Testament we see glimpses what that cure is. Moses raises up a snake on a pole, which absorbs the poison and the curse that the Israelites are experiencing. The snake, which is the emblem of evil, is hung up and takes the sin from the people. We see God here offering a way out.

The earth and his people may be cursed, but God is a God who wants to reverse the curse. And when Jesus comes, the beautiful truth is that he comes to reverse the curse on every level. Jesus said, 'The thief comes only to steal, kill and destroy. I have come that they may have life, and have it to the full.'

And how does he do this? By becoming the one lifted up like the snake on a pole. The one who will break the power of evil by his sacrifice. In John 3:14 he makes this explicit, 'Just as Moses lifted up the snake in the wilderness, so the Son of Man must be lifted up, that everyone who believes may have eternal life in him.'

Here is the crux of today's sermon, the thing that I really hope enters into our souls: The solution is more profoundly beautiful and loving, more powerful and definitive than anything the curse can do. Because the level at which Jesus entered into all the twisted and warped pain of the universe was more than we could have expected or hoped for.

As I was trying to reflect on how I could get across what this is saying about what happened when Jesus was lifted up I thought of a couple of examples. I don't know if you have seen 'The Green Mile' in which an innocent death row convict called John Coffey, note the initials, has this amazing ability to absorb other people's illnesses and bring healing. At one point he literally sucks out the badness from the prison governor's wife and she is immediately healed. He on the other hand experiences her pain. When Jesus was lifted up, then, did he similarly *absorb* the effects of the curse? Did they fall onto Him so that He experienced them, and so He might deliver us? Yes - it's true. And for him to do that for you and for me is surely as loving a gift as we could expect. Surely it's as beautiful a sign of God's profound love for us as we could ever have hoped for. And yet Jesus did more.

I also thought by way of illustration of the story of Maximilian Kolbe, a Polish priest imprisoned at Auschwitz, who famously took the place of a man who was going to be executed. He gave his life for another. He took the curse, if you like, of the man's fate. If this too was illustration of what Jesus did in being lifted up on the pole what an amazing testimony to the love of God. He deflects the power of the curse onto himself. He willingly gives up His life for you and for me. And yet in being raised on the pole Jesus did even more than this in breaking the power of the curse and in showing God's love for us.

The picture of the snake on the pole tells us that even more happened here. And the clue is in Galatians. Referring to those who are struggling under the curse of constant inability to keep God's law and all the anxiety, divineness, and fear that's associated with it, Paul writes, 'Christ redeemed us from the curse of the law *by becoming a curse for us*, for it is written:

'Cursed is everyone who is hung on a pole.'

He didn't just absorb the effects of the curse. He didn't only deflect the effect of the curse. *He became the curse.* In His own being, in His own essence, God became His opposite. He became twisted, warped, distorted into everything He wasn't. He became his antithesis. It wasn't a lamb on the pole or on the cross. It was a snake. Jesus embraced the curse of being God's enemy. That's how much He loves you. 'Father, I will become everything I am not. I will become the opposite of everything you intend. I will accept spiritual death, the light of your love being turned off in me.'

The depth of the curse needed a more profound love to defeat it. A love that would not just *absorb* it but would *become* it.

That is our Saviour. The Son of Man lifted on the pole, cursed for us, wearing the thorns of a broken creation on his head. Yes, that's a deliberate echo of what happened to the world in the beginning.

Jesus wasn't just cursed; he became the curse. And by doing so he didn't just address our behaviour, but the very core of who we are. God now doesn't just look the other way from the curse in us, He makes us into something entirely different. Paul puts it like this, He who knew no sin *became sin for us*, that we might *become the righteousness of God.*

As profoundly as Jesus became the curse, so profoundly you and I have become his righteousness.

And just as we earlier addressed the idea that God the Father can come across in the Old Testament as less than He is, we need to understand that the Father was just as broken and wounded by the curse as the Son. Jesus did not become the curse so that God could vent his rage, but so that God could set the world right by overcoming sin and evil. God became His own opposite because of His love for us.

We are works in progress, who we are is yet to be fully realised. But there is no one here today who lives under the curse any more. He became the curse for us and for his resurrection breaks its power forever. When we see the snake, may we once again be drawn in wonder and love to the Saviour who shows us just how far He will go and just how much we are worth by becoming everything we never thought He could be.

The Beginning of The Cross

Why have you forsaken me?

Psalm 22
Guy Donegan-Cross. 11th February 2018

Psalm 22 is one of the darkest points of the whole Bible, and it's obviously the psalm that Jesus quoted when he was in despair on the cross. It teaches us much about the relationship that God wants with us and what real faith is.

But before we get into that it's worth noting the amazing relationship between the psalm and Jesus' experience. If you bear in mind that the psalm was written over 600 years before Jesus' death and compare some of the verses in it with the record of what Jesus experienced there is an incredible prophetic witness to the cross. If you're someone who is exploring faith it's just worth asking yourself how you respond to this.

Psalm 22 (written at least 600 years beforehand)	Matthew 27
1 My God, my God, why have you forsaken me? Why are you so far from saving me, so far from my cries of anguish?	46 About three in the afternoon Jesus cried out in a loud voice, 'Eli, Eli, lema sabachthani?'(which means 'My God, my God, why have you forsaken me?')

7 All who see me mock me; they hurl insults, shaking their heads. 8 'He trusts in the Lord,' they say, 'let the Lord rescue him. Let him deliver him, since he delights in him.'

41 In the same way the chief priests, the teachers of the law and the elders mocked him. 42 'He saved others,' they said, 'but he can't save himself! He's the king of Israel! Let him come down now from the cross, and we will believe in him. 43 He trusts in God. Let God rescue him now if he wants him, for he said, "I am the Son of God."' 44 In the same way the rebels who were crucified with him also heaped insults on him.

15 My mouth is dried up like a potsherd, and my tongue sticks to the roof of my mouth;

48 Immediately one of them ran and got a sponge. He filled it with wine vinegar, put it on a staff, and offered it to Jesus to drink.

16 Dogs surround me, a pack of villains encircles me; they pierce my hands and my feet. 17 All my bones are on display; people stare and gloat over me. 18 They divide my clothes among them and cast lots for my garment.

John 19:23 When the soldiers crucified Jesus, they took his clothes, dividing them into four shares, one for each of them, with the undergarment remaining. This garment was seamless, woven in one piece from top to bottom.

On the cross we hear Jesus calling out, 'My God, my God why have you forsaken me?' He entered into the opposite of all that He was made to be -loved by His Father forever. He experienced in the depths of His being complete separation from the love of the Father.

So where was the Father? An angry God who despised his son? A strange God with a split personality?

The reality is that although Jesus experienced what it feels like to be in hell -which is literally to be cut off from God's presence - the Father was as much part of this as the Son. In Saint Andrew's Church in Salzburg there is a sculpture of Jesus on the cross. But if you look closely you can see that He is being held by the Father and the Spirit. This is a mystery, but it's an important mystery for us to understand. God was not removed from Jesus' suffering. We read in 2 Corinthians that God was 'in Christ reconciling the world to Himself.' The whole of God suffered. And as a result, God, uniquely out of all religions, experiences the pain of humanity in Himself. God is on the inside of our suffering. Of your suffering. He knows what god forsakenness feels like!

Writing from his Nazi prison cell a short time before his execution, a 38-year-old pastor the name of Dietrich Bonhoeffer said this: 'Only a suffering God can help. What help can an emotionless God who cannot suffer be to a suffering people? But God does suffer, with us and for us.' Jesus wept. He bled. He cried out in pain. And God who made us love us so much that He became his own opposite in that pain. So if you are suffering today the revelation here is that God is on the inside of your pain and knows it. What an amazing mystery!

And Psalm 22 reveals to us what real prayer and real faith is. Sometimes we think faith is carrying on in the face of difficulties as if they are not there. Sometimes we think faith is not having any questions or complaints. But here is the truth: good Christians know how to complain. In fact if you never complain to God, the probability is that you don't have a real relationship with Him.

On the most recent U2 album there is a line that shocked me. 'Oh Jesus, if I'm still your friend, what have you done for me?' In fact, the language is a bit stronger than that. Strong enough to make me sit up and take notice. Here is someone telling Jesus that He has let him down. In another psalm they sing, 'Wake up, dead man.' Where are you?

The Psalms contain about 40% of what we call lament. Complaint. Anger. Sometimes at God. Believe it or not in the Bible God commends people who are authentic, gutsy, and not pious-sounding. If you read the book of Job you hear a man who will not pretend that he is happy with God. Three friends try and persuade him to stop being, in effect, so rude. But in the end God tells them to be quiet – Job's speech is honest and authentic. And that's what God wants. CS Lewis once wrote, 'The first prayer we can pray is this: may it be the real me speaking to the real you.'

There is a strong theme running through the Bible that being willing to honestly struggle with God lies at the heart of true faith. For modern people we sometimes think faith means having psychological certainty about God. For the Jews who prayed Psalm 22 it was something different. Faith wasn't about clinging to a feeling of certainty. Faith was about keeping trust in God even in the faith of uncertainty. Look at Jacob wrestling with the angel. That's faith. The kind of relationship that is solid enough to know that God can handle his complaints, confusions and accusations. That's why I say good Christians know how to complain.

This helps is in two ways. Firstly, when you're with someone who is suffering and you don't know what to say. We are too quick sometimes to try and rush to resolution. To try and say something that will sort it out. Actually, real faith allows people to express their grief. Sometimes if we don't just sit and listen then we are not doing the Christ-like thing. I heard someone say recently, 'It's always necessary to speak the truth in love, but it's not always necessary to speak.'

And the second thing is that for us feelings of doubt, struggle, and despair can be part of our faith, not separate from it.

Genuine faith can be complaint expressing itself. Our culture wants us to be authentic. And so does God. He can take it. I'm convinced actually that the reason some people drift away from God is because they think they can't be themselves before Him. They hit a rough patch and don't know how to process it. We have to help one another to know that we can cry out, 'My God, my God why have you forsaken me?'

In the Scriptures when people were in despair they sometimes used to tear their clothes. This was just a physical expression of what they were feeling inside. Today you've been given a piece of cloth. If there is something that you need to get off your chest with God and you don't know how to express it, sometimes doing something physical can help. I invite you to sit in God's presence and when you're ready to tear the cloth if you need to. It might help you speak as the real you to the real God. May we all grow in being able to pray as Jesus did on the cross.

Jesus' suffering on the cross was immense - more than we can understand. The depth of god forsakenness. We need to know that this changed everything. There is another passage in scripture which, like Psalm 22, can be easily seen as fulfilled in the new Testament. Isaiah 53 prophesied about one who

was despised and rejected by mankind,
    a man of suffering, and familiar with pain.
Like one from whom people hide their faiths
    he was despised, and we held him in low esteem.
4 Surely he took up our pain
    and bore our suffering,
yet we considered him punished by God,
    stricken by him, and afflicted.
5 But he was pierced for our transgressions,
    he was crushed for our iniquities;
the punishment that brought us peace was on him,
    and by his wounds we are healed.
6 We all, like sheep, have gone astray,

each of us has turned to our own way;
and the Lord has laid on him
    the iniquity of us all.

Why did he suffer so terribly? Out of love, and so that we can be embraced and loved by God for ever. Because of Jesus we have peace. By his wounds we are healed. And whereas He experienced god forsakenness in a way that is unimaginable, because of Jesus no one can snatch you out of the Father's hand. You will never be forsaken. Your future is certain, your present is held, your past is dealt with. May you know the beauty of the cross.

The Words of The Cross

'Father, forgive them, for they know not what they do.'
'My God, my God, why have you forsaken me?' 'I thirst.'
'Father, into your hands I commit my spirit.'
'Woman, here is your son...Here is your mother.'
'It is finished.'

The Words of The Cross

'Father, forgive them, for they know not what they do.'

Luke 23:34
Dan Watts. 18th February 2018

On the cross, God, the Immortal, the great I Am, who came to us in the flesh, was put to death. As Jesus hung on the cross he spoke and prayed. These were the last words of a dying man, the seven sayings of Christ on the cross:-

Father, forgive them (Luke 23:34)
My God, my God, why have you forsaken me? (Matthew 27:45-46)
I am thirsty (John 19:28-30)
Father, into your hands I commit my spirit (Luke 23:44-46)
Woman, behold, your son (John 19:26-27)
It is finished (John 19:28-30)
Today you will be with me in paradise (Luke 23:39-43)

In Richard III, Shakespeare wrote 'The tongues of dying men--Enforce attention like deep harmony--Where words are scarce--They are seldom spent in vain--For they breathe truth--That breathe their words in pain.'

These words are important, they go to the very heart of who Jesus is. Two of the seven statements Jesus made on the cross, deal specifically with the subject of forgiveness. There are hundreds of principles Jesus taught during His time on earth. As He was dying, He could have reiterated any of those things. Yet, He spent two of the seven things He said on the issue of forgiveness.

Here was a moment of grave injustice, the sickest, most twisted moment in all of human history as man put God to death. We would expect that in a moment of such injustice, in a moment of such extreme suffering, a person would cry out for vengeance. 'Father, strike them down!' 'Father, don't hold them guiltless!' But Jesus cries out forgiveness. 'Father, forgive them, for they know not what they do.'

God knows how deeply we struggle with the idea and concept of forgiveness.

How difficult it is for us to know we are forgiven? A man I met this week is dying of cancer and has a few months to live. He knew he would be meeting God soon, but he was living in fear and guilt. He was afraid of what would happen when he meets God. He had the wrong picture of God – he thought he was going to be punished for his sins and so was gripped with fear.

God knows this about us. He knows how difficult it is for us to forgive those who have wronged us. He also knows how difficult it would be for a lot of us to believe God could forgive us, because of how often we've wronged Him.

This is why Jesus spent two of the seven things He said on the cross about forgiveness.

Jesus offered His prayer to those who did not know what they were doing.

'Father, forgive them, for they know not what they do.'

It wasn't offered to those who were repenting, confessing and sorry for their sins. The Bible says that while we were still God's enemies, He offered us forgiveness. Not after we've realised our wrongdoing and sinfulness, but while we were still dead in our transgressions and sins, He offered us mercy and forgave us.

It's not our confession and repentance that births God's mercy, but it's God mercy that births our confession and repentance. God acts first. We act second. It's not that we first loved God. He first loved us.

In light of this how should we forgive?

Many times, our willingness to forgive is directly tied to the other person's ability to know what they've done. We're willing to forgive just as long as we see this person truly knows how badly they've messed up. We're willing to forgive as long as we see the sorrow and remorse they are feeling. But not before then.

If that were the way God viewed forgiveness would there be any salvation for us? If the only way God would forgive us, is if we truly realised the enormity of our sin, showing remorse and sorrow, confessing and repenting just the right way, would there be any forgiveness and salvation for us? No.

So Jesus prays, interceding for us, not just when we're repenting, but especially when we're not. Especially when we don't know the enormity of how we've wronged Him and are not confessing.

Are you called to forgive those who have wronged you and either don't know it, or don't care? Yes, because that's when God forgave you. You didn't know the enormity of your sinfulness or how to confess nor did you want to. You didn't know how to repent nor would you ever try to. You were His enemy and wanted nothing to do with Him. In the midst of you wronging Him every chance you got, God offered you mercy and forgave you.

Jesus prayed for forgiveness for us, not when we were sorry for our sins, but when we were happy in our sins.

There are a lot of us who have the hardest time wrapping our minds around God just wiping clean a person's slate. It just doesn't make sense. I suspect there are many of us who carry a sense of guilt and shame. You don't believe God could actually forgive someone like you. We don't think God would offer forgiveness to a person who keeps failing like we do.

Your salvation is not based on what you've done. It is a gift of God.

There are some of you here are thinking I don't understand the injustice done to you. Someone has abandoned, abused or ruined your life. They've cheated on you, divorced you. You have a legitimate complaint. Right now, as you sit, you still bear the scars and consequences of that injustice. I'll never know or understand.

But somebody does. Somebody knows the level of injustice you've felt. Somebody else still bears the scars of the consequence of that injustice. Jesus.

You'll never look more like Jesus then when you experience a radical injustice and you breath out radical forgiveness. That's when you know the gospel of Jesus has truly taken root in your life and heart.

Radical injustice met by radical forgiveness.

Right now in your life, are you harbouring any bitterness and anger against someone who did you wrong? Do you wake up in the morning with hatred in your heart towards someone? If you do, this morning is the perfect time to let go of your bitterness and anger and forgive the person who has treated you badly.

But you may want to say, 'But Dan, they don't deserve to be forgiven.' But I say, 'Did the people who put Jesus to death deserve to be forgiven? No. 'Do we deserve to be forgiven by God when we sin against Him? No. Yet God still forgives us. We must forgive because God forgives us.

Leonardo da Vinci painted the fresco 'The Last Supper' in a church in Milan. Two very interesting stories are associated with this painting.

At the time that Leonardo da Vinci painted 'The Last Supper,' he had an enemy who was a fellow painter. da Vinci had had a bitter argument with this man and despised him. When da Vinci painted the face of Judas Iscariot at the table with Jesus, he used the face of his enemy so that it would be present for ages as the man who betrayed Jesus. He took delight while painting this picture in knowing that others would actually notice the face of his enemy on Judas.

As he worked on the faces of the other disciples, he often tried to paint the face of Jesus, but couldn't make any progress. da Vinci felt frustrated and confused. In time he realised what was wrong. His hatred for the other painter was holding him back from finishing the face of Jesus. Only after making peace with his fellow painter and repainting the face of Judas was he able to paint the face of Jesus and complete his masterpiece.

One of the reasons we may have a hard time accepting the forgiveness of God is that we find it hard to forgive others. That's why Jesus said, 'If you forgive men when they sin against you, your heavenly Father will also forgive you.' (Matthew 6:14-15) If you want your relationship with Jesus to be all that it should be, forgive your enemies and do all you can to demonstrate Christ's love to them.

I realise that at times, it is hard to forgive...but we must. We must forgive so that we can get on with our lives. At this moment, if you need to forgive someone, do what Jesus did, pray, 'Father, forgive them.'

The Words of The Cross

'My God, my God, why have you forsaken me?' 'I thirst.'

Matthew 27:46-49, John 19:26-28
Guy Donegan-Cross. 25th February 2018

It's a real paradox that at the moment when Jesus has most given up His power that in some ways He seems most in control. He cries out the first line of a Psalm, 'My God, my God why have you forsaken me?' seeming to deliberately be finding prophetic roots of His own suffering. Then we read in John that, 'knowing that everything had now been finished, and so that Scripture would be fulfilled' – there was a deliberate plan which was now complete - He said, 'I am thirsty', and someone offered him vinegar on a sponge. In doing so even they, unwittingly, at that moment fulfilled a scripture from Psalm 69, 'I looked for sympathy, but there was none, for comforters, but I found none. They put poison in my food and gave me vinegar for my thirst.' Even though giving him the drink is not an act of compassion but an act of mockery, it is still part of the plan. Jesus seems to be supremely aware that He is participating in something that has already been written. Something far more significant than meets the eye.

But you will sometimes meet people, or you may even feel yourself, that even though Jesus may act as though He is fulfilling something greater, the fact is that this is the ignominious death of an insignificant preacher in a backwater 2000 years ago. Just another crucifixion. Just another misunderstood person. Atheist commentators and others may find it hard to believe that Christians could place so much importance on one small event.

They may even say something like this. 'This doesn't sound like true history -after all they are obviously quoting from so many previous sources in such a way that it sounds like a constructed story. It sounds like somebody has put together various bits and pieces from here and there and tried to make what was a relatively common event into something bigger.' In fact, they might go on to say that there are lots of stories about gods who die and rise again from around this time. And so it's plain that someone has been influenced by these and superimposed them onto the story of Jesus.

These are fair points, and worth looking at. The way in which the accounts are written is obviously drawing attention to other things. So they are partially right - there is some construction here. But the idea that Jesus' death is therefore actually a legend, influenced by the myths of gods such as Osiris, Mithras or Dionysus who allegedly were all born of virgins, all martyred and all resurrected is not credible. For a start, within these parallel stories often there is no actual death or resurrection of a god in the first place. In addition all of these legends with the exception of Osiris were written after the birth of Christianity. As well as this, Jewish writers would have found the idea of referring to pagan stories repulsive. The main point though is that these ancient myths, which after all may be tapping into something which is inherent in human nature in their desire for redemption, almost always refer to gods who die and are reborn in the same way that seasons come and go. As Tom Wright says these stories are not about resurrection from the dead and a new world being born, but more about fertility rites and the soil being good for planting. So in these stories gods died and rose every year.

If you look more specifically at the Osiris story you read that he was killed by his brother, chopped up into 14 pieces and scattered throughout Egypt. Isis then rescued all but one of his body parts, reassembled them and brought him back to life. He was then given leadership of the underworld. The claim that this account parallels the Jesus story is quite a stretch. And it's not even a resurrection account since Osiris was never fully put back together and remained in the realm of the dead. So in the limited sense that these stories contain a vague intuition that death must be defeated by a god there is a parallel, but other than that there's nothing relevant or direct. Jesus' death and resurrection is not just another mythic construction.

Nevertheless, there are elements of construction in the telling of it. It's quite clear from all the accounts that Matthew, Mark, Luke and John deliberately interweave references from other places in such a way that they are explicitly pointing them out to the reader. They are not just giving the facts of what happened, although that is part of it, but they are unveiling the significance of it. And they're doing so not because they need to make something up, but because they want us to know that this is far more than an insignificant preacher in a backward country being given a common death. This is, in fact, the moment when everything that God wants to do is fulfilled.

And in these two phrases, 'My God, my God why have you forsaken me?' and 'I thirst' they are showing us that in this event that looks so ugly, so pathetic, so tortuous, is the revelation of the height, depth, breadth and length of the most unimaginable love there is.

When Jesus cries out, 'My God, my God, why have you forsaken me?' He is crying out the most painful words in history – a primal scream at the heart of all things. But some of us might say, 'How can this be a loving God? To allow His child to suffer like that? I would never even do that to another person's children, let alone my own.' On the surface, it sounds like God is more into abusing his own Son, than revealing love.

Yet can you cope with another paradox? On the cross, when God descended as far as He could go from who He was, He was revealing who He truly is. The agony of experiencing his own godforsakenness was the truest expression of self-giving, total, other-centred agape love that you will find nowhere else but on Calvary. Jesus' scream of abandonment was the expression of a God who was not going against His own nature on the cross, but expressing His nature. For God is nothing but love – love that is found in three persons who eternally give themselves to each other, pour themselves out for each other. Love that is most fully expressed in denying Himself for others. In giving Himself for others. And so what greater love could there be then to pierce His own heart, to stoop down and experience the very opposite of all that He is.

When He cried out, 'Why have you forsaken me?' Jesus revealed the love of the Father, the Son and the Spirit, at an intensity nothing else could reach. He came to the furthest extreme possible out of love for a race of rebels who wanted only to crucify him. The gospel writers don't include this because they want to construct a clever myth. They include it because on that small hill in that backwater Love was finally revealed.

This is the depth of God's love for you. The Son willingly embracing the agony of separation, the Father and Spirit willingly bearing the grief. And doing so not with any regret, or holding back, but because that is who they are. Love, love and love.

To the bystanders those last words, 'I thirst,' were the pitiful cry of a lost child in His final moments – and they would have been right. But those who see the love of God revealed also know they are the final cry of a God who thirsts for one thing – to be united in love with His creation. God thirsts for you and me. We may long for Him, search for Him, yearn for Him. But He thirsts today for your love, your heart, your trust. And even if when He calls you put the vinegar of rejection to His lips, what will He continue to do? To love you. Forever. Because that is who He is. This is a story no human being could construct. This is a love that calls us beyond ourselves, to a place where we will know we are never forsaken, and will never be thirsty again.

The Words of The Cross

'Father, into your hands I commit my spirit.'

Luke 23:43-49
Guy Donegan-Cross. 4th March 2018

In facing that final moment of death, last words can be quite revealing.

George Orwell's last written words were, 'At fifty, everyone has the face he deserves.' He died at age 46. And I am 50 this month! Hmmm...

But more inspiring is the true story told in a film called 'Of Gods and Men' about a group of seven Catholic Cistercian monks living in Algeria in the 1990s during the Algerian Civil War who knew that they would almost certainly be murdered if they stayed, yet voted and decided to remain with the people they believed that Jesus had called them live amongst. Sure enough, men with guns came in the night, and they were all kidnapped in March 1996 and found dead in May that year. A letter was found written by the Prior, Christian de Cherge, and it began with these words: 'Should it ever befall me, and it could happen today, that I am killed as a victim of the terrorism swallowing up all foreigners here, I would like my community, my church, my family, to remember that my life was given to God....for this life lost, I give thanks to God. In this 'thank you,' which is said for everything in my life from now on, I certainly include you, my last-minute friend who will not have known what you are doing...I commend you to the God in whose face I see yours. And may we find each other, happy 'good thieves' in Paradise, if it please God, the Father of us both.'

Where did he get the strength to leave these beautiful words, to die with such courage? Surely he was echoing his Saviour, learning how to die from Jesus. Jesus' last words in John are 'It is finished.' And here in Luke, 'Father, into your hands I commit my spirit.' In saying this he is again quoting a Psalm, this time Psalm 31. Every moment is significant. And in these words we find the last words for every Christian.

We read that Jesus cried out these words with a loud voice. Could it have been with effort? The sheer pain and exhaustion of the journey? Because in thinking about our dying words, or perhaps recalling those whom we have lost, let's remember that Jesus wept at death. That He was afraid in the garden. We want to learn how to face death, how to live with it, but please be reassured that as a Christian you are not required to be in denial of the sadness, difficulty and effort that dying can entail. You are not required to be superhuman. God knows death is an enemy to be defeated, an alien intrusion which we struggle with. Just as our first birth can entail much effort, mess and pain, sometimes our being 'born again' will be a journey that requires much effort. We may cry out in a loud voice. Jesus did. And God will hear and understand.

But perhaps His loud voice was also one of determination. A sense of finally being able to surrender with the conviction that everything was done, and everything was all right. A loud voice of effort, but not of fear.

Jesus died well. I've always been struck by John Wesley's quote, 'Our people die well.' Henri Nouwen writes of us being able to 'befriend' death, and that the way in which we face our death can be one of the greatest gifts we offer to our loved ones, and in which we can glorify Him. I always do this with some trepidation, because when you are accompanying someone who is dying you are treading on holy ground you have yet to walk on, but as a Christian brother I will always try and encourage my brothers and sisters who are dying to see it as a gift they can offer, and a way of glorifying God.

Of course if we know our death is soon, or if we have lost a loved one, we will grieve. But Paul wrote this, 'Brothers and sisters, we do not want you to be uninformed about those who sleep in death, so that you do not grieve like the rest of mankind, who have no hope.' There is a world of difference between hopeful grieving, and hopeless grieving. For Jesus, death was the greatest effort, and yet, in these final words we see His total ability to surrender in hope and trust.

When our time comes, our birthright as Christians is to face death like this. How?

In these final words, Jesus inserted one word that makes all the difference. The Psalmist said, 'Into your hands...' Jesus said, 'Father, into your hands...' For Jesus, in life, His Father was everything. And in death, the Father was home. When we face death, it no longer matters who we are, what we have done, whether our moral stocks and shares are up and down, whether we have lived a relatively good or bad life compared to the person next to us. It only matters to whom we belong. 'Father, into your hands...' We belong to God – that is all that matters. And His hands are greater than death.

A few weeks ago my Gran died. She was 97 and in the last phone conversation we had she said she just wanted to be with Jesus. She was a committed Roman Catholic all her life, and the funeral service was held in a Roman Catholic church in Yeovil. The style was a little strange for me, but what struck me was how little the priest said about my Gran's life. But how much he said about who she was in Jesus. So the coffin was covered first with a baptism cloth, to remind us that what most mattered about my Gran was that she was baptised into Jesus, and that her physical death was just a transition in a journey which began when she was baptised into Christ. Then a crucifix was placed on her coffin, to show that the most significant thing about her was that Jesus had died for her. Then a Bible, which spoke of the fact that it doesn't particularly matter what the world says about you, but what God says about you....Of course we talked about her and celebrated her, but the final word is...she belongs to God. When you die, what matters is that you are in Christ, that your life is held in Him, that He is Lord. When I surrender to the giver of life, I can commend myself to Him in death.

Knowing whose we are is the key. But we are also to know what happens after death. Jesus, for the joy that was set before Him, endured the cross. It was knowing what was coming that gave Him the strength to endure. Notice Paul wrote, 'Brothers and sisters, we do not want you to be uninformed about those who sleep in death.' Genuine hope has genuine content. What is our hope beyond death? In the simplest terms, what happened to Jesus after death is the pattern of what will ultimately happen to us. Resurrection! A transformed yet bodily existence in a new heavens and renewed earth. Not spirits or souls floating on a cloud, but recognisable people of body, mind and spirit, fully liberated from death and living in His presence. Our whole selves restored in a way that completes God's dream to be at one with His creation.

That's the ultimate promise. It's no wonder Paul says, 'For me to live is Christ, to die is gain.' He so looks forward to the future promise that he feels really ambivalent about waiting. He is living in that Clash song, 'Should I stay or should I go?' and says, 'I am torn between the two: I desire to depart and be with Christ, which is better by far...' We used to sing a song with a rather jolly tune with these words...but they made it sound a pedestrian hope. For the Christian, to die is GAIN. I don't know, but maybe Steve Jobs glimpsed this. According to his sister Mona, the Apple founder's last words were, 'Oh wow. Oh wow. Oh wow.'

Just a further bit of detail. Paul writes about those who have fallen asleep in Christ, who will later be changed. So there are two stages after death. Those who have already died are 'asleep' waiting for the final resurrection. And then when the last trumpet shall sound God will renew all things in the final resurrection. We symbolise this all the time. May they rest in peace...and then rise in glory. Two stages. At a remembrance service we play the last post and flags go down...into sleep...and wait, and then as the 'Reveille' plays (which means 'Wake Up!') the flags go up. So, although life after death will be unlike anything we experience, what we are taught to hope is that our immediate experience is rest – peace, an end to suffering, and wholeness in God's hands.

Billy Graham once said, 'Some day you will read or hear that Billy Graham is dead. Don't you believe a word of it. I shall be more alive than I am now. I will just have changed my address. I will have gone into the presence of God.' I heard another Christian writer called Dallas Willard interviewed about his impending death due to cancer. He spoke bravely acknowledging his fears about the process, but said that when he died he wasn't even sure he would notice at first. That he might look back after a while and realise something had changed. The truth is that for Christians we are already dead. We went down into the waters of baptism, we shared in Christ's death, dying to ourselves, and rising to new life with Him, sharing in His resurrection, being assured of eternal life which begins now. We simply are waiting to change address. And when we are already dead, what can we chase after that is worth anything other than the love and purpose of God? And when you are waiting for this glorious future, why worry about so many of the things that preoccupy us? And why fear?

The Coptic Christians of Egypt have been suffering terribly at the hands of Islamic terrorists. Last year 21 Christian men were led out and beheaded. A priest was brutally murdered, and there have been numerous bombings. And a man called Faheem took the blast of a bomb in his church and saved many lives in the process. Afterwards, his wife said this. 'I'm not angry at the one who did this, I'm telling him, "May God forgive you, and we also forgive you. Believe me, we forgive you. You put my husband in a place I couldn't have dreamed of."' Orthodox priest Boules

George said this: 'I long to talk to you about our Christ, and tell you how wonderful he is,' said George, addressing the terrorists. But then turning to the church, he said, 'How about we make a commitment today to pray for them?'

Those people know that Jesus took away the sting of death. They know whose they are, they see the promise of what's to come, and know that those who have already died and are waiting to change address cannot be harmed. And so every day, until their last day, they are willing to pray, 'Father, into your hands we commit our spirits.'

John Wesley also said, 'Every Christian should be ready to preach, pray or die at a minute's notice.' May we be ready to die well, to His glory. Can I offer you two responses? As a Lent discipline, if you haven't done it already, why don't you plan your funeral? I've provided a template of ideas, and if you want us to have it in the safe for when the time comes we can keep it here. But here is a prayer you can begin each day of your life with: 'Father, into your hands I commit my spirit.' So that when the day comes that our bodies fail, our whole selves may glorify Him in a loud voice.

Name **Funeral Plan**

I want my body to be buried/cremated
I want my ashes scattered at:
I want this kind of coffin:
I want people to wear:

I want my funeral to be called a

I want this to be the message and tone of the funeral

Music to play in the service

Songs/hymns to sing

Bible reading(s)

Other reading(s)

I'd like this to happen afterwards:

I want a collection for:

Signed and dated:

The Words of The Cross

'Woman, here is your son...Here is your mother.'

John 19:25-28
Dan Watts. 11ᵗʰ March 2018.

Jesus made seven statements while He hung on the cross. They were the dying words of Jesus; each one has significance and meaning. They teach us something about the heart of God.

While being crucified, Jesus looked down and saw His mother and His disciple John. He looked at Mary and said, 'Woman, behold, your son. John is now your son. And John, this is now your mother.' Mary went to live with John for the rest of her life.

At first glance this statement doesn't seem to compare to some of the weightier ones that Jesus made. It feels like a side note where Jesus is just taking care of some family business. Yet, the more I look at it, I realise this is a moment that has real theological and practical significance for our lives.

Jesus was being incredibly intentional with His words and actions to give us a glimpse into the heart of God.

In order to understand the significance we must consider the situation in which He was saying it. The final scene in Jesus' life on the hill of Golgotha - Mary, his mother was there, of course, standing at the foot of the cross. You can imagine the anguish she felt watching the suffering and death of her son, unable to lift a finger to help him. Standing beside her was his beloved disciple, John: powerless to do anything, watching the death of his closet friend, master and leader.

Jesus was paying for the sins of the world.

He was suffering one of the most painful experiences of physical torture that any person could possibly endure. He had been whipped and tortured, and nailed to a cross. He was naked and humiliated; he was suffering insults and abuse. But the physical and mental cost was nothing compared to the spiritual cost He was paying. Jesus had existed eternally with the Father in a holy, loving and sinless relationship. Everything had been amazingly perfect between them until this moment. For the first time in eternity, sin entered into their relationship that had never been there before. The relationship Jesus had enjoyed forever was ripped from Him. This was a massive cost Jesus was paying.

Jesus was performing the most significant act in human history. Yet, suddenly in his last moments, Jesus called to her and said, 'Woman, behold your son.' Then he called to John and said, 'Behold, your mother!' He stopped to make sure a desperate widow had somebody to take care of her.

Jesus was always doing stuff like this, feeding the hungry, stopping to heal the woman in the crowd suffering from bleeding, caring and loving the ignored and forgotten like Zacchaeus. What He did wasn't always necessarily significant. But when He chose to do it was.

Jesus could have done this the night before while in the Upper Room. He could have leaned over to John and asked him to take of His mother right there. He could have done if after He had died and risen from the grave. He spent a lot of time with both Mary and the disciples before He ascended to heaven. But He didn't. He chose the moment when He was hanging on the cross, paying for the sins of the world, to stop and take care of Mary's future.

This was the only statement Jesus made that didn't have to be said while on the cross. The other six statements were absolutely unique to the cross being either a direct fulfilment of prophecy that had to take place during the death of the Messiah or was Jesus responding to a very unique situation.

However, Jesus knew the cross was coming. He could have taken care of Mary's need at any other point of His journey. So why did He choose to do it while on the cross?

Jesus was revealing something to us. He was letting us see a view of God's heart most of us would have missed otherwise. It's a beautiful picture of how God actually loves us. God doesn't just care for and love you by offering you salvation. He wants to love you and care for you even in the smallest details of your life.

A lot of us need to see this and understand the depth of God's love for us. As He's shedding His blood for the sins of the world, showing us He can meet the most significant need in the universe – paying the price for our sin, He's also showing us He's not too busy, too tired or too distracted to care for one desperate widow who needs to be taken care of in her old age: a woman who needs a roof over her head and food to eat, a woman who needs a home.

The word of Jesus to his mother from the cross is a great encouragement to our faith. For if he could provide for his own, in the moment of his deepest weakness and humiliation, how much more can he meet all our needs today: resurrected and ascended and seated at the right hand of God full of power and glory. He loves and cares for us in the big things, but also the smallest details of who we are.

Jesus intentionally chose this moment to speak these particular words. It was no accident. Not only was he revealing his love and care for you in the small details of life, he was also instituting the way that would be experienced. One of the gifts Jesus gave to us from the cross was the church: a loving, caring, sustaining, encouraging family beyond family.

This scene at the foot of the cross, teaches us what it means to live in communion with others. From the cross, Jesus turns us outward toward people to whom we are not physically related, identifying these people as our spiritual mothers, fathers, sisters or brothers. From the cross, Jesus breaks down the barriers between people and creates this new family by the power that flows from his death for humanity. On the cross Jesus is redefining what it means 'to be a family'. These two individuals who might have been abandoned, forgotten, left alone, are knit together into a new family. They are the first family of what we know was to become the early church.

This new reality, this new kind of family, would play an integral role in continuing Jesus' mission in the world. We find Mary and John among those gathered in the Upper Room when the Holy Spirit is given to the Church.

The cross broadens the concept of family - the family of God. Jesus changes the basis of relationships. No longer are relationships to be formed on the basis of natural descent, on shared ethnic identity, on agreeing that others are 'like us.' Our shared place beneath the cross is the only foundational space for relationships from now on. This new family or new community exists entirely so we may love Jesus and love one another. Jesus teaches us to love, even when he is dying, even when we are dying. That is what relationships are about, and that is what the cross is all about.

Dietrich Bonhoeffer's understanding of Christian community is 'that we belong to one another only through and in Jesus Christ'. Jesus is at the centre of all Christian community; it is He that binds us together. He is the focus and the purpose for meeting together as Christians. Bonhoeffer's bold conclusion is that we need each other in order to experience Jesus and grow as Christians.

In the New Testament there are 100 'one-another' statements. One third of these focus on unity, how the Church is to get along. One third focus on love, the nature of relationships between each other. Paul wrote Two thirds of these commands, and four of these commands are about kissing! What is interesting is that only a handful of theses commands/statements can be carried out within a large group setting. Almost all of these commands can only be carried out in a small family like community.

Perhaps there is a sense in which the church today needs to further embrace or rediscover Bonhoeffer's radical theology that led to such an important view of Christian community. Our Christian growth and formation is intrinsically linked with our participation in a family community group.

Beneath the cross of Christ, Christian fellowship is born not just for Mary and John, but also for you and me, and for everyone else who believes, for all who believe.

Beneath the cross of Christ, we become a new family.
Beneath the cross of Christ, we become brothers and sisters in Christ.
Beneath the cross of Christ, we realise that we are now part of the family of God.

On the cross, Christ entrusts us as his children to one another, to love one another.

The Words of The Cross

'It is finished.'

John 19:28-30
Stewart Davies. 18th March 2018

Before we get into what this word from the cross says to us, let's briefly deal with what it doesn't say!
It does not tell that Jesus said 'I am finished!' It was not a cry of defeat, of a man who had given up on what he came to do…

In Saturday Night Fever, a minor part is Tony's brother, Father Frank Junior, who quits the priesthood. The reason Father Frank junior quit, he says was this: 'One day you look at a crucifix, and all you see is a man dying on a cross.' I'd say it would be a decent guess that for most of the audience watching Saturday Night Fever back in the seventies, eighties, this was a sentiment they recognised, empathised with: 'you look at a crucifix, and all you see is a man dying on a cross.'

The Bible does not tell that Jesus said 'I am finished!' Jesus' word from the cross 'tetelestai' (Greek – Τετέλεσται) means not 'I am finished', how Father Frank Jr had come to see it, but 'It is finished!' 'It is accomplished!' 'It is completed!' 'It is all done!' From the cross, his body failing, his mind wracked with agony, the dying Jesus proclaims fulfilment, not failure! Not the cry of a man who had given up on what he came to do – emphatically the opposite – 'it is all done'!

What do you wish Jesus had done before he died? Written down all his words and thoughts in a single book? Killed all the bad guys? Done a sign that could never be doubted by anyone, so that everyone would be Christian? Eliminated world hunger?

I heard a presentation the other week which put this so straightforwardly – shall we say in plain Yorkshire - I had to take notes: 'Jesus lived a full life. He discharged fully his duties to man and to God. He was not willing to die and leave anything undone that he ought to do'.

This is not an open question in John's Gospel, we're not left to wonder if Jesus has left anything out – because we have that word from the cross '*tetelestai*': It is finished! It is all done!

It's good to recall from time to time that reading our Bibles a verse, a section, a chapter at a time, can mean we miss the message. There's real benefit in getting a view of an entire book, to understand not just sections but the message that the inspired writer has fashioned for his reader in its entirety.

So, when we open up the whole of the Gospel of John, we see this bigger picture, how he has set out for his readers the progressive steps that Jesus made toward ensuring that his work was complete.

Like all the best school text books – the answer is at the back! John says very plainly what the purpose of this book is, the big picture that he hopes his Gospel will convey:

'Now Jesus did many other signs in the presence of his disciples, which are not written in this book. But these are written so that you may come to believe that Jesus is the Messiah, the Son of God, and that through believing you may have life in his name.' (John 20:30-31)

John sets out in his Gospel that the work of Jesus on earth was God's amazing mission to bring all people back to himself, their loving heavenly father, in order that they have life in all its fullness.

The signs and wonders Jesus performed were not showy stunts of power to grab attention and court followers, indeed John rather understates the drama of the miracles. Rather, they were specific signs of how God deals with all that prevents us from entering into the life he intends for us; how God in Jesus - fully human - breaks the cycle of human failure, sickness and death; how God is welcoming each and every person into this new life in Jesus. Nothing less than a New Creation breaking through, with the power of the Creator demonstrated through signs and wonders, in human life transformed.

'The works that the Father has given me to complete, the very works that I am doing, testify on my behalf that the Father has sent me.' (John 5:36)

Let's take a moment to stand back and see how John's Gospel makes this clear. Just like the seven days in the Genesis account of Creation, biblical scholars find in John's Gospel seven signs in Jesus' earthly ministry, bringing about the new relationship between God and his people, the new Creation.

And in setting this out for the reader, John highlights each of the signs that Jesus did, showing God's immense power coming together with his amazing vulnerability to effect his loving purpose. No less than bringing women and men into abundant and eternal life as God's New Creation.

Product placement alert! The choir that Richard Paul, Frances Bryant, Toby Donegan-Cross and I sing in – is performing an amazing piece next Saturday evening at St Peter's: it's called 'In the Beginning' with music by the American composer, Aaron Copland, and the words by no less than King James VI!

And you've guessed – 'In the Beginning' is the creation story from the first two chapters of the book of Genesis. Each new creation day's wonders are conveyed with exhilarating music – interspersed with a chanted.. 'and the morning and the evening were the [1st, 2nd etc] day'. Like some Gregorian timepiece counting the days! And the piece makes tangible how each day is more wonderful, climaxing with the God's creation of his beloved partners in creation – humans – on the sixth day. But, it's not finished on that sixth day. God's work of creation finished on the seventh day when God rested. (Genesis 1:31, 2:1-2)

Now I've said that biblical scholars find in John's Gospel seven signs in Jesus' earthly ministry, bringing light and life from God to humankind, the new Creation. Now, the mention of 'biblical scholars', should give you the heads up that not all is going to be plain and simple - and I rely on our learned friend N T Wright for this listing - but it starts off clearly enough.

1. John 2 – turning water into wine
    'Jesus did this, the first of his signs, in Cana of Galilee, and revealed his glory; and his disciples believed in him.' (John 2:11)

2. John 4 – healing the son of the royal official
    'Now this was the second sign that Jesus did after coming from Judea to Galilee.' (John 4:54)

3. John 5 – healing the man by the pool in Jerusalem
    'But Jesus answered them, "My Father is still working, and I also am working."' (John 5:17)

4. John 6 – feeding the huge crowd
    'When the people saw the sign that he had done, they began to say, "This is indeed the prophet who is to come into the world."' (John 6:14)

5. John 9 – healing the man blind from birth
    'Never since the world began has it been heard that anyone
    opened the eyes of a person born blind. If this man were not
    from God, he could do nothing.' (John 9:32-33)

6. John 11 – raising Lazarus from death to life
    'This man is performing many signs. If we let him go on like
    this, everyone will believe in him.' (John 11:47-48)

Six amazing signs in ten chapters of John's Gospel (2-11),
climaxing at the sixth sign – the raising of Lazarus to life – how
could there be more, what could out-do the raising of a dead
man!

And indeed the next chapter, the twelfth chapter of John's
Gospel, is pivotal: impending struggle and death are spoken
about plainly alongside the popular climax of the ministry of
Jesus as the crowds came out to meet his entry into Jerusalem.

So, John 12 puts alongside each other"

'It was also because they heard that he had performed this sign
that the crowd went to meet him. The Pharisees then said to one
another, "You see, you can do nothing. Look, the world has gone
after him!"' (John 12:18-19)

with

'Jesus answered them, "The hour has come for the Son of Man to
be glorified. Very truly, I tell you, unless a grain of wheat falls
into the earth and dies, it remains just a single grain; but if it
dies, it bears much fruit."'(John 12:23-24)

Six signs are done, the seventh sign is about to begin.

To complete his work, Jesus faced giving himself over, in a final
sign that it is clear that he dreaded...

'Now my soul is troubled. And what should I say—'Father, save me from this hour'? No, it is for this reason that I have come to this hour.' (John 12:27)

'Am I not to drink this cup that the Father has given to me? (John 18:11)

To complete his work, the signs of God's new creation, Jesus had to go into a situation that he dreaded.

He submitted himself to the scheming of Judas and the pharisees

He handed himself over to his enemies, allowing no resistance when they came to arrest him.

He was an object of the political whims of the local tinpot rulers, the jealous religious leaders, the nervy Roman governor – his back flayed viciously, that not enough, sentenced to be tortured to death on a cross

He was made to appear in a ghoulish auction, in front of a crowd who chose a murderous brigand to live in preference to him – Barrabas!

He became vulnerable to the rank and file too. See how the soldiers treated their meek captive, a plaything for a boring Thursday night shift, the worst of human nature, cruel for the fun of it

He was humiliated - stripped naked on the cross, his agonising death was watched for entertainment by the jeering crowd.

Jesus had taught his disciples to pray 'Father, don't bring us to the time of trial but deliver us from evil', yet handed himself over to trial and submitted himself to the power of malevolent people.

And yet, and yet. John would have us understand that by this 'handing over of himself', humbled even to death on a cross, Jesus fulfilled, finally and gloriously, what he came to achieve.

Tetelestai, the shout from the cross – it is all done!

The seventh sign of John's gospel - finishing the work of Jesus, God in Christ bringing life in all its abundance – is the passion of Christ. We use the word 'passion' to describe the events of this seventh sign – the passion of Christ. We do this because the word comes from *'passus'* meaning an object of, dependent on, the action of others.

By contrast, in the first six signs, Jesus is the subject of actions – he is the one in control! So, we read in John's Gospel that: Jesus *directs* the stewards to serve the water as wine; Jesus *announces* that the dying boy will live; Jesus *instructs* the cripple to stand and walk; Jesus *distributes* the loaves and fishes to feed the crowd; Jesus spreads mud on the blind man's eyes so he sees; Jesus *commands* the dead Lazarus to come out of his grave.

But in the final sign of John's Gospel, the passion of Jesus, he hands himself over, becoming the object...

the soldiers, their officer, and the Jewish police *arrested* Jesus and *bound* him; one of the police standing nearby *struck* Jesus on the face; Annas *sent* him bound to Caiaphas the high priest.; The officials *took* Jesus from Caiaphas to Pilate's headquarters; Pilate *summoned* Jesus ; Pilate *took* Jesus and *had him flogged*; the soldiers wove a crown of thorns and *put it on his head*; and the soldiers *dressed* him in a purple robe; Pilate *handed* him over to them to be *crucified.*

Are we able to comprehend that God in Jesus chose to become vulnerable to, dependent on his creature, man? That the work of Jesus was not complete until he became the object of human decision and deeds – handed himself over, even to death?

Are we able to comprehend such love, that God in Christ did not stop at those signs of power and authority that drew the crowds to follow, but went all the way to give himself over to human choice, ultimately to rejection by those same crowds, to cruelty from of those he subjected himself to?

And can we comprehend that in this is glory?!
'Jesus answered them, "The hour has come for the Son of Man to be glorified."' (John 12:32)

John's Gospel tells us clearly that the glory of God is to be seen supremely in Jesus handing himself over, becoming passive, subject to the will of others – for mercy, for acceptance, for denial, for bullying, for injustice, for cruelty, for slaughter. Glory?!

'Now my soul is troubled. And what should I say—"Father, save me from this hour"? No, it is for this reason that I have come to this hour. "Father, glorify your name." Then a voice came from heaven, "I have glorified it, and I will glorify it again."' (John 12:27-28)

W. H. Vanstone writes 'of all that God has done in and for the world, the most glorious thing is this – that He has handed Himself over to the world, that He has given to the world not only power of being but also the power to affect himself – power of meaning. Of such a nature is that ultimate dimension of divine glory which is disclosed in the handing over of Jesus.'

St Paul writes (Philippians 2:8-9) 'he humbled himself and became obedient to the point of death -even death on a cross. Therefore God also highly exalted him and gave him the name that is above every name.'

'The passion of Jesus was not his human misfortune: it was the decisive manifestation of his divinity.'

The word of Jesus from the cross – *tetelestai* - 'it is all done' - is our evidence that Jesus saw it to fulfilment.

And what is God saying to us in this, here, today?

Jesus said 'It is all done' – and there's a message here for you who need to make sense of your life in your **Heart** – where you make tough decisions.
You've found a place in this community but you've not yet decided if you are willing for it to be 'you'.

You've heard the call to love the Lord your God, to walk in all his ways, to keep his commandments, and to hold fast to him, and to serve him with all your heart and with all your soul ... but you've not yet let this have a claim on your heart.
You've felt stirred at times, dared to believe that this might be what it means for you to 'come home'.

Let the Passion of Jesus - the cross it's thorn-crowned fulfilment - appeal to you now.

Jesus gave himself over to death that you can enjoy life in all its abundance, starting today.

Hear him speak your name, '[ ] will you accept all I have done for you and hold fast to me, serve and follow me with all your heart, walk in my ways all your days? Then come'.

Jesus calls out 'IT IS ALL DONE' for you. Now is the time to come, take up your cross and follow him.

Jesus said 'It is all done' – and there's a message here for you who need to make sense of your life in your **Soul** – where you check that you are following on the right way.

Are looking to make sense of experiencing a season of *Passus,* waiting, as a patient, on the margins?

You are left aside from action, from decision; you are dependent on actions and decisions of others.

You wait to know if you will receive care or neglect, be noticed or ignored, be valued or bullied.

How is God in this? Where is God in this? Let the Passion of Jesus affirm you in this place, today.

For Jesus, becoming an object of, dependent on, the actions, ignorance and cruelty of others, was the fulfilment of glory and God was glorified in it and through it all.

This is where God is, for you who wait, who suffer – right here – declaring for all the world and all time that becoming vulnerable, waiting – was God's supreme way of loving us: and saying to you: receive this season of Passus as a treasure from God to be lived and offered back to God in trust.

'IT IS ALL DONE' is his call to you, through the waiting, the pain and tears, to know his glory as you follow him through this season of your life.

Jesus said 'It is all done' – and there's a message here for you who need to make sense of your life in your **Mind** – where you check the consistency of what you hear and see and know to be true.

Is understanding the cross proving to be an obstacle in your journey of faith. Is your intellect stuck in the gym of theory rather than out on the journey of faith?

Paul, in what we can read in his letters to young churches, is disarmingly honest about the way that the message of the cross is received by many 'For the message about the cross is foolishness' to many. Yet it is powerful, life changing and true to us (1 Corinthians 1:18).

However rigorous or knotted up our thinking may be, as we work out what the cross means, Jesus's final word 'It is all done' is a word to us. Let this word speak to you, challenging you to make the intellectual step, to move forward to employ your mental powers on living faithfully and abundantly.

'IT IS ALL DONE' is his call to you to accept his work as complete, take up your cross and follow him and prove in your life, as of so many questioners through the centuries and around the world: Christ the power of God and the wisdom of God.

Prayer

Lord Jesus. You emptied yourself of everything but love – all for me - to ensure that 'it is all done'. I have come to believe that you are Lord, and through believing we have life in your name. Let me not hold anything away from your love – my heart, my soul and my mind – all for you. Amen.

The Narrative of The Cross

We are the Crowd: Palm Sunday
Transfiguration and Prediction
Passover and Communion
Gethsemane and Calling
Failure is not Final: Peter's Betrayal
'The Kiss of Betrayal'
Challenging the myth of Redemptive Violence
Jesus before Pilate
'Do not weep for me.' Things that Knock you Sideways
Torn Curtain and Centurion's Recognition.

The Narrative of The Cross

We are the Crowd: Palm Sunday

Luke 19:28-40
Guy Donegan-Cross. 25th March 2018

Before we get into the meat of the sermon have you ever
wondered if Jesus knew somehow supernaturally that the
donkey would be available or if it was just something he had
arranged before? Or why Jesus needed to ride on a donkey that
hadn't been written before? Or what this whole event on Palm
Sunday was saying about who he is?

To be honest the question about whether Jesus had some kind of
supernatural affinity with the owner of the donkey doesn't really
matter that much - on the edge of towns in those days you would
quite often find places where you could rent donkeys for
journeys. It could even have been that the donkey was called
Uber. What is significant that for our purposes is that the donkey
haven't been ridden before. In the Old Testament things that
hadn't been used previously were special - they weren't normal
everyday things, they were reserved for worship, for serving
God. By ensuring that this donkey hasn't been ridden before
Jesus is telling us who he really is - this colt is reserved for none
other than Yahweh, coming to do fulfil his mission.

But even more profoundly, by riding into Jerusalem on a donkey
when he could've so easily walked, Jesus is deliberately fulfilling
a prophecy from Zechariah, written between 550 and 548 years
before. The people of Israel were waiting for the Messiah to
arrive. And in chapter 9 of Zechariah we read,

'Rejoice greatly, Daughter Zion! Shout, Daughter Jerusalem! See,
your king comes to you, righteous and victorious, lowly and

riding on a donkey, on a colt, the foal of a donkey ... He will proclaim peace to the nations.'

Further on in chapter 12 we read also that the Messiah would be one who would be pierced:

'And I will pour out on the house of David and the inhabitants of Jerusalem a spirit of grace and supplication. They will look on me, the one they have pierced, and they will mourn for him as one mourns for an only child, and grieve bitterly for him as one grieves for a firstborn son.'

He would come in victory, and he would come in suffering. And Jesus fulfilled both of those. Deliberately.

And as he comes into the city people put coats before him - as they would have done those days to honour conquering heroes - but more significantly they sing Psalm 118. The crowd seems to understand what is going on here. That Psalm is a Psalm for the honouring of the King who would approach the temple and be blessed by the priests. As Jesus passed by the crowd would be singing, 'The Lord is God, and he has made his light shine on us. With boughs in hand, join in the festal procession up to the horns of the altar. You are my God, and I will praise you; you are my God, and I will exalt you.'

So the unridden donkey, the Zechariah prophecy, and the Psalm say exactly who Jesus is. And the Pharisees don't like it. That's why they say to Jesus, 'Teacher, rebuke your disciples!' Don't you know what they are saying about you're here? But Jesus is having none of it. He is owning who he is. 'I tell you,' he replied, 'if they keep quiet, the stones will cry out.' If people don't recognise Yahweh, because they are harder than stones, then the creation will.

But... you know how the hymn goes. 'His sweet praises they sing, resounding all the day Hosannas to their King... then Crucify! is all their breath, and for his death they thirst and cry.'

Within a week these same people are turning on Jesus. Why? Because in their eyes he has failed. The king who will liberate them has been arrested.

How fickle they are, aren't they? Saying one thing one day, and then so quickly abandoning it? They like the Zechariah 9 Jesus, but don't seem to have read chapter 12. They don't seem to understand what God is really doing. Jesus has not met their expectations. He has let them down. And so they so quickly give up on him.

Fortunately, you and I are not like that, are we? Our commitment to Jesus stays firm. We would not have abandoned him so easily. Would we?

The truth is not only is it easy for us to judge them with the benefit of hindsight, but actually when it comes down to it this crowd is too easily us. Too easily me. Too easily you.

Maybe we will love Jesus if everything is going as we want it? As long as he meets our expectations?

And I wonder, what kind of heart do you and I really have? Robert Redford was walking one day through a hotel lobby. A woman saw him and followed him to the elevator. 'Are you the real Robert Redford?' she asked him with great excitement. As the doors of the elevator closed, he replied, 'Only when I am alone!'

What are we like when we are on our own, with God?

Or just on our own, behind, for example, the wheel of a car? I once heard of someone who said, 'I don't know what it is, but when I am in my car, I can find myself saying things and I just don't know where they come from... It's like another person takes over, not the real me...' but, the truth is, that person behind the wheel, that is precisely the moment when the real you is most revealed.

There was a zoo that was noted for their great collection of different animals. One day the gorilla died, and to keep up the appearance of a full range of animals, the zookeeper hired a man to wear a gorilla suit and fill in for the dead animal. It was his first day on the job, and the man didn't know how to act like a gorilla very well. As he tried to move convincingly, he got too close to the wall of the enclosure and tripped and fell into the lion exhibit. He began to scream, convinced his life was over... until the lion spoke to him: 'Be quiet, or you're going to get us both fired!'

The crowd is there to remind us that if we really want to follow Jesus then the best spiritual discipline we can have is to take off the mask that highlights the difference between who we know we are called to be and who we actually are. To embrace our own hypocrisy.

Before getting to why that could be actually a wonderful thing, I want to share a story I like. Donald Miller, a student at a liberal arts college in America, decided to take the mask off in a big way by setting up a confession booth in the middle of the campus and wearing a monk's outfit. But the question is, who was confessing to whom? In walked his first customer, Jake.

'So what is this? I'm supposed to tell you all of the juicy gossip I did at Fresher's Week, right?' Jake said.
'No.'
'Okay, then what? What's the game?' he asked.
'Not really a game. More of a confession thing.'
'You want me to confess my sins, right?'
'No, that's not what we're doing.'

'What's the deal, man? What's with the monk's outfit?'
'Well, we are, well, a group of Christians here on campus, you know.'
'I see. Strange place for Christians, but I'm listening.'
'Thanks,' I said. He was being patient and gracious. 'Anyway, there is this group, just a few of us who were thinking about the way Christians have sort of wronged people over time. You know, the Crusades, all that stuff ...'
'Well, I doubt you personally were involved in any of that, man.'
'No, I wasn't,' I told him. 'But the thing is, we are followers of Jesus. We believe that he is God and all, and he represented certain ideas that we have sort of not done a good job at representing. He has asked us to represent him well, but it can be very hard.'
'I see,' Jake said.
'So this group of us on campus wanted to confess to you.'
'You are confessing to me!' Jake said with a laugh.
'Yeah. We are confessing to you. I mean, I am confessing to you.'
'You're serious.' His laugh turned to something of a straight face.
'There's a lot. I will keep it short,' I started. 'Jesus said to feed the poor and to heal the sick. I have never done very much about that. Jesus said to love those who persecute me. I tend to lash out, especially if I feel threatened, you know, if my ego gets threatened. Jesus did not mix his spirituality with politics. I grew up doing that. It got in the way of the central message of Christ. I know that was wrong, and I know that a lot of people will not listen to the words of Christ because people like me, who know him, carry our own agendas into the conversation rather than just relaying the message Christ wanted to get across. There's a lot more, you know.'
'It's all right, man,' Jake said, very tenderly. His eyes were starting to water.
'Well,' I said, clearing my throat, 'I am sorry for all that.'
'I forgive you,' Jake said. And he meant it.
'Thanks,' I told him.
'You really believe in Jesus, don't you?' he asked me.

'Yes, I think I do. Most often I do. I have doubts at times, but mostly I believe in him. It's like there is something in me that causes me to believe. I can't explain it... What do you believe about God?' I asked him.

'I don't know. I guess I didn't believe for a long time, you know. The science of it is so sketchy. I guess I believe in God though. I believe somebody is responsible for all of this, this world we live in. It is all very confusing.'

'Jake, if you want to know God, you can. I am just saying if you ever want to call on Jesus, he will be there.'

'Thanks, man. I believe that you mean that.' His eyes were watering again. 'This is cool what you guys are doing,' he repeated. 'I am going to tell my friends about this.'

'I don't know whether to thank you for that or not,' I laughed. 'I have to sit here and confess all my crap.'

He looked at me very seriously. 'It's worth it,' he said. He shook my hand, and when he left the booth there was somebody else ready to get in. It went like that for a couple of hours. I talked to about thirty people, and many people wanted to hug when we were done. All of the people who visited the booth were grateful and gracious. I was being changed through the process. I went in with doubts and came out believing so strongly in Jesus I was ready to die and be with him.

I think that night was the beginning of a change for a lot of us.

There is something good about embracing the fact that we are as fickle, broken, hot and cold, spiritually weak as anyone in that crowd. Blessed are the poor in spirit, said Jesus. For a start, it releases us from the burden of being a hypocrite. Because, as soon as you admit to your hypocrisy, you stop being one! You are free. Paul even said, 'I will boast of my weaknesses...' because his need to perform had been replaced by something deeper. Knowing he was loved, whatever.

Owning who we really are as well means that we will stop judging one another. As Christians we have absolutely no right to judge anyone for anything. Jesus made that abundantly clear.

Especially those outside the church family. A healthy heart considers others better than ourselves. When we know we are the crowd, we will bear with one another. Yes, we may disappoint each other. But, because we know who we are, we bear with it. Yes, we hurt each other sometimes, we misunderstand each other. But that is what families do. And the love of Christ compels us to forgive, and forgive and forgive.

Do you want an honest, real, raw heart before God and other people? Can I encourage one practice and one attitude shift? The practice is this: the Bible says 'Confess your sins to one another, that you may be healed.' In the Catholic church, you confess to a priest. And if that is what you need, then as one hypocrite to another, I'm happy to listen. But can we offer each other maybe in twos or threes, or in our communities, a place where we can lay down the burden of our contradictions and sins, and make God's forgiveness real to each other? So much depression is caused by people carrying stuff around inside. It's God who does the forgiving, but it's your family that can help you experience it. What, or who might you need to confess to, in order to be healed?

And be reassured by this. Jesus let the crowd get him totally wrong, but he still went with them. He still loved them. He knew their hypocrisy, but he bore with them. He allowed them to misinterpret him completely. To totally misunderstand him. As, in fact, he often does throughout the whole Bible. He could have called them out and said, 'Hang on, haven't you read the whole of Zechariah?' But he didn't. The truth is, He allows you and I to get him wrong again and again and again. And why? Because he knows us – He knows who we are when we are behind the steering wheel, on our own, when all our pretences are stripped away. He knows our incomplete understanding, our downright stupid ideas. And He doesn't care. All he cares about is that we trust in His love, and that we might see it more clearly. He will never let go of a hypocrite he died for. Here's a true King and Messiah for everyone.

The Narrative of The Cross

Transfiguration and Prediction

Matthew 17:1-23, Matthew 20:18-19
Rachel Tunnicliffe. 8th April 2018

If you are a teenager, or you've been one, or you've ever dealt with one, you will be familiar with the cry, 'You just don't get it!' When someone doesn't understand us, we feel frustrated, angry, let down, unloved, and often, we think it's not worth the bother of trying to explain, we just give up (or storm off) and leave the misunderstanding unresolved. If you're the one being accused of 'not getting it', it's tempting to lose patience and give up trying to get it. Not being understood is frustrating. Not understanding can be bewildering. Neither is good for making the relationship stronger. It says in Proverbs 4:7 in all your getting, get understanding. Understanding each other is what builds relationships.

Our sermon series now and in the coming weeks is about Jesus and the cross, which is good, because as we all know, the cross is at the heart of our faith in Jesus. It's also good, because it might be just me, but I think the cross is one of the hardest things to understand fully. We all know the story of what happened at Easter, that Jesus died on the cross to pay for our sins, so we could have a relationship with God. But really 'getting' how that works and what it means and why it had to be that way can be really confusing. Throughout Christian history it's been called a mystery. We all like a mystery (I'm particularly keen on Murder She Wrote, or Inspector Morse) but when we think about the cross and realise that we don't fully get it, it can be unsettling and frustrating. Sometimes we can want to give up trying to understand it all and back off. That probably isn't good for our relationship with Jesus. Thankfully, Jesus never runs out of patience with us; His love never runs out; His faithfulness never ends.

In our readings today we see Jesus and the disciples struggling with this very thing. In the chapter of Matthew's gospel just before our reading, Jesus has been explaining to his friends the disciples what's going to happen: 'From that time on Jesus began to explain to his disciples that he must go to Jerusalem and suffer many things at the hands of the elders, chief priests and teachers of the law, and that he must be killed and on the third day be raised to life.' (Matthew 16:21) The disciples didn't get it. Peter in particular got cross and said that mustn't happen. Jesus got a bit frustrated with him and told Peter he wasn't helping because: you do not have in mind the things of God, but the things of men. He knows Peter doesn't understand, but Jesus doesn't run out of patience. He doesn't give up on his friends.

As we heard in our reading, Jesus takes Peter, James and John up a mountain and they have another opportunity to understand what He has been saying to them and who he truly is. These three best friends of Jesus see him transfigured – changed, so that His face shone like the sun and his clothes became as white as light. And as if that wasn't amazing enough, Moses and Elijah appeared and were talking with Jesus. And then a bright cloud covered them, and a voice from the cloud (God's voice) said,' This is my Son, whom I love: with him I am well pleased. Listen to him!'

Wow! These three men have seen with their own eyes a glimpse of Jesus' glory, a clue of what He will be like when he's been raised from the dead, an indication that God is in charge and all will be well. These three men have heard with their own ears God's own voice telling them Jesus is his son. These three Jewish men have seen Moses, from whom their people received God's laws, and the prophet Elijah, as a clue that Jesus fulfils both the law and the prophets. With this amazing experience, surely they get it now? Jesus told them, and now he has shown them too; they have heard and seen and experienced.

Well, when they come back down the mountain, Jesus heals a boy who the disciples haven't been able to heal. You can sense Jesus' frustration when he says, 'O unbelieving and perverse generation, how long shall I put up with you?' He tells the disciples it's their lack of faith that stops them being able to heal the boy. They go to Galilee and he tells them again, 'The Son of Man is going to be betrayed into the hands of men. They will kill him, and on the third day he will be raised to life'. He has told them straight. Again! Do they get it now?

Obviously not, because not long after this, on their journey to Jerusalem, Jesus takes the disciples aside and says to them, 'We are going up to Jerusalem and the Son of Man will be betrayed to the chief priests and the teachers of the law. They will condemn him to death and will turn him over to the Gentiles to be mocked and flogged and crucified. On the third day he will be raised to life!' Jesus tells them again, this time with a little more detail, and again he offers them the reassurance that despite the awful things that will happen to him, God is in charge and all will be well, because on the third day he will be raised to life.

We sense Jesus' frustration but we see his patience. He doesn't give up on these men who never seem to get it. He keeps telling them, he explains, he goes to great lengths to help them understand. He knows their limitations but he faithfully persists. He tells them in straight words what's going to happen, he demonstrates who he is through the power of his miracles, he reveals or shows his glory by letting them experience that transfiguration, giving them a glimpse of how the Jewish history they would have known all comes together in him. He even tells Peter, James and John not to tell anyone what they've seen until after he's been raised from the dead – he knows they need time to develop their understanding and that the rest of the people are not ready for this yet. He knows them and he loves them and he knows what they can and can't cope with. He never runs out of patience; his love never runs out; his faithfulness never ends.

It can seem strange to us that these close friends of Jesus didn't get it – they knew their scriptures telling of the coming Messiah, they had followed Jesus closely and seen him perform countless miracles, they had heard his parables and his teachings, they had heard him tell them straight about his death and resurrection, and they had that amazing transfiguration experience. But I wonder if we would have done any better? We have the whole of the Bible including 4 gospel accounts of what happened and the letters of Peter, James and John explaining it all. We have the benefit of hundreds of years of clever scholars and vicars explaining things to us, books and films, the explanations and testimonies of the experiences of other Christians, and still our understanding is limited. It says in 1 Corinthians 13:12 'Now I know in part; then I shall know fully. We won't fully get it until we meet Jesus face to face.'

In the meantime, we can be encouraged by Jesus' patience with the disciples and how that worked out. Look at John's gospel, where John explains so beautifully for all our benefit who Jesus is and says, 'The Word became flesh and made his dwelling among us. *We have seen his glory*, the glory of the One and Only, who came from the Father, full of grace and truth.' John's experience and his understanding, when he finally got it, there for all time and all people to help our understanding. And look at Peter in the second chapter of Acts, just a fisherman, after Jesus' death and resurrection, full of the Holy Spirit, explaining to a crowd of people from all sorts of countries clearly and confidently about what had happened, and how it fitted into the context of the scriptures and God's plan for his people. And look at what Peter wrote in his second letter: '...we were eye-witnesses of his majesty. For he received honour and glory from God the Father when the voice came to him from the Majestic Glory saying, "This is my Son, whom I love; with him I am well pleased." We ourselves heard this voice that came from heaven when we were with him on the sacred mountain.'

Isn't it amazing that Jesus knew how much his friends could cope with and when? And the way they shared their understanding and their experience has helped the people they came into contact with and generations after them to understand and know Jesus.

So where does that leave us with our struggles to understand? I hope we can all be reassured that however old or young we are, it's ok if we don't fully understand, it's normal. In fact, anyone who claims to fully understand everything about Jesus and the cross is probably missing quite a lot. Be reassured that however little we understand, Jesus never runs out of patience; his love never runs out; his faithfulness never ends. So we shouldn't give up either.

Our understanding can develop through studying the Bible, through hearing or reading about other people's thoughts and experiences, through prayer, through nature, through dreams and pictures that God may give us, and many other ways at different times in our lives. I help in the morning children's groups and recently the year 3 and 4 children have been thinking about Jesus being the good shepherd and us being like sheep, needing his protection and provision, and understanding how the good shepherd loves his sheep so much he's willing to lay down his life for them. In all our children's groups we learn together and help each other's understanding develop through teaching, drama, games and all sorts of fun combining showing and experiencing as well as telling. Those of you not fortunate enough to be involved in the children's groups might develop your understanding through your communities meeting during the week and hopefully know that for adults just as for children, experiencing and seeing are just as important as hearing and telling. Just occasionally something in a church service might strike you as helpful. Last week I watched the film of The Shack, from the book by John Paul Young. It's a story written after the author felt God had given him a way of illustrating the relationship between God the Father, Jesus and the Holy Spirit in a way that might be helpful. I found it really moving and both the book and the film in different ways have helped me develop my understanding a little more. That author, like countless others, was prepared to share what God had shown him, trusting it might help others develop their relationship with Jesus.

So I hope you can relax and know that it's ok not to understand everything. Our loving God knows what we can cope with, and when we are ready for more – he knows you and loves you and is prepared to meet you where you are and move at your pace. He never runs out of patience; his love never runs out; his faithfulness never ends. From that place of being relaxed, there are two things I'd like us to think about now:

The first one is this: what might Jesus be wanting to show you or tell you now? What glimpse might he be wanting to give you to build your understanding and your relationship with him? What message of encouragement or challenge might he be wanting to offer you? Are you open to that? If you are, ask him. And then watch out for him answering, because he will, whether you are young or old, whether you know a lot or a tiny bit, he always has more to give you when you're ready. It could be something he will tell you directly or something he will show you through a situation or an experience. Look and listen and wait for a word, a picture, an understanding, a gift.

The other thing I'd like us to think about is whether we can all be a bit more like Jesus in the way we deal with each other. When there's a misunderstanding, whether you're frustrated that someone doesn't get you, or you're losing patience with someone, could we be a bit more patient and loving and faithful instead of being tempted to give up or storm off? Jesus never runs out of patience; his love never runs out; his faithfulness never ends. Let's ask that by the power of his Holy Spirit living in us, we could be a bit more like that.

The Narrative of The Cross

Passover and Communion

Matthew 26:17-30
Guy Donegan-Cross. 15th April 2018

As Rachel was saying last week, really getting to grips with what the cross means can be a journey for us and we don't always get it. But God knows how we tick and communicates with us in ways that we can experience as well as understand. For example, human beings like stories - and the whole Bible is a story. Human beings like to be in relationship - and Jesus came to have a relationship with us as a human being. And human beings love eating - and God is so gracious that He has given us a meal so that, while we might not understand everything completely, we can experience it in our very selves.

So as Jesus headed towards the cross there's a story and a meal that help us get into the mystery of what was going on. Jesus used an old story and an old meal to show his disciples exactly what he was going to be doing.

The story began many, many years before Jesus came. It was the story of a people - the Israelites - who had been slaves in Egypt for 400 years. They were under bondage, captivity. They could not be the people they were made to be. They were oppressed, made to create bricks all day, despised. But God raised up Moses to lead them out so that they could worship him in freedom. Moses challenged Pharaoh to let God's people go but again and again Pharaoh refused. Every time he refused God sought to persuade him by challenging his power. But Pharaoh would not let the people go.

Eventually this led to something terrible. God allowed the destroyer to challenge Pharaoh's power by striking down the first born in Egypt. On one night death would come to every family in the land, striking down the first child.

But God gave his people away out of death. He told them to kill a lamb or a goat, it had to be unblemished, to eat it in a hurry, and to put some of its blood on the doorposts of their houses. When the destroyer approached and saw the blood covering the family, it would pass over them – they would escape death.

Well this was a terrible night. The Israelites were delivered but Pharaoh was finally persuaded to let them go. They had to leave quickly though. They started baking bread but they were in such a hurry that they didn't have time for it to rise. So they just took flat bread - what we call 'unleavened' bread - with them. And you know the story. They came to the Red Sea which parted, and they escaped through to freedom.

This story is a picture of what God wants to do for us - to lead us into freedom. Freedom from death, from sin, from bondage. This was the most special day of God's people's lives. And so he gave them a special way to remember it. A meal. A meal at which they were told the story of what God had done to remind themselves of who they were and who He was. And a meal at which they would celebrate and laugh and joke because He had set them free. It would also be a meal when they could be sorry for all the pain that was caused. It was a Passover meal.

What did they eat? Well, obviously they ate lamb. But they also ate bread which had not risen - which they called matzoh. And at one point in the meal they would break the bread in half to represent the lamb which was broken and whose blood saved them. The broken body of the lamb reminded them that they had escaped death.

But even better than that they would drink wine. Four cups of wine - each with a different meaning. The first cup was called a cup of sanctification - which means making something special. It was a reminder that this was a special meal. The second cup was the cup of sorrow, when they remember all the pain that they had been through and all the pain of the world. Then they would eat the meat and the bread and after supper they would drink the third. The third was called the cup of redemption. It was a cup that celebrated that they had been brought out of slavery into freedom. And finally they would finish with the fourth - the cup of completion. They were still waiting for that day when they would be totally free. They had got out of Egypt but the fourth cup was about longing for that day when they would be in the promised land. So the meal did two things. It looked backwards to when they had been brought into freedom, but also forward to when they would receive all that God had promised.

This meal was celebrated every year by the Jewish people and still is today. God commanded them to eat it, because He really wanted them to remember what he had done. He said, 'The whole community of Israel must celebrate it.' And it's a meal that Jesus celebrated just before he was crucified. Why did he do it then and what happened when he did?

Let's read about the meal and see what Jesus made of it. (Matthew 26:17-30)

So here at the Passover the disciples were remembering with Jesus how as a people they had been brought out of slavery, how death had passed over them, and how they were longing for the completion of all that they had done. In view of the fact they hadn't really understood what was going to happen to Jesus in the coming days, they must've been totally shocked when Jesus took the bread, the matzoh which represented the broken lamb and instead said to them. 'This is my body.' In other words, 'I am the lamb.' The broken one who will rescue you from death. And this is a new covenant. This is different. Because before it was just for one group of people at one time. But when death passes into me it will pass over all people. I will break the power of death for everyone by my body broken. No one need to be afraid of death any more. Later on in the Bible we read, 'For Christ, our Passover lamb, has been sacrificed.'

And then, later on in the meal, we read that, 'after supper he took the cup and said, 'This is my blood shed for you.' Which cup was this in the meal? It was the third - the cup of redemption. Jesus was saying, 'It's my blood that will redeem you. That will liberate you from slavery, from bondage, from sin, from Satan.' And again, whereas in the first meal The Israelites celebrated being led out from slavery under the Egyptians, now Jesus was saying through His blood there would be a way for all people to be led out from slavery for ever.

So every time we share in Holy Communion we are actually sharing in the Passover meal as redefined by Jesus. A meal which says to us that God has done everything to bring us freedom from death, from sin, from bondage for ever. It's a costly meal though. Killing a lamb can make us slightly squeamish, but it cost God the death of His firstborn. Death passes over us because it didn't pass over Jesus. He embraced it in order to break its power forever.

So let's finish by reflecting on taking communion. God is so good. We might not get Him completely, but he gets us. He knows that we need stories and meals to get under the skin of what He's about.

Whereas for Jesus and his first followers sharing bread and wine always took place with a small group of people you knew over a meal, for us it's become rather more formal. We get together, we tell the story, but the whole tangible remembering is really helped by being a family together, communing with God and with each other. In our church a few of us have been given the job of leading this meal, and there are certain boundaries about the way it is done – and I guess part of that is about protecting it in some way – but if you are in a community or group and would like to share in the meal at home, then please always ask because that is something we can offer.

Let's get away from the idea as well that it is like magic. It isn't. You don't need to have communion to get close to God. His presence is with you. He is always there, closer than your skin. It is an incredibly special gift that God has given us this way of knowing Him, but if we find ourselves in a place when we can only feel closer to Jesus if we have communion, then we are getting closer to superstition than to worship. I think of it like kissing my wife. I don't need to kiss my wife to show her that I love her. I don't need to be kissed to know that she loves me. But sometimes, it helps. It's a sign of the relationship that is always there. Imagine if you met me and I was crying, and you asked me why and I said, 'Well, my wife hasn't kissed me for six hours and so I don't know if we are married any more.' That's a bit like saying, 'I can't love Jesus, serve Him or be close to Him, unless I've had communion.' The mark of a disciple isn't how often you take part in a meal.

Can I address another question? Sometimes people don't think they are good enough, or believe enough, to join in with the meal. This is sad for two reasons. Firstly, did you notice how Jesus shared this meal with Judas, whom He knew was about to betray Him? There is always a place at Jesus' table for everyone. And do you know where the Israelites were when they first started celebrating this meal? They were in the wilderness. Wandering around for forty years. Yes, they had got out of slavery, but they were still waiting for God's Promised Land. And every year, they would look backwards to what God had done, and look forward to what He was going to do.

And that's where we all are isn't it? We all know that because of Jesus death has passed over us. Hallelujah! We have been set free. Hallelujah! But aren't we all still waiting for the final completion? Still longing for that day when we will see God face to face, in His Promised land? Don't you long for that? So, when you come to the meal, you come as an incomplete Christian, knowing that you in many ways you are still in need of being made into what God wants. You live between the cup of redemption and the cup of completion. And it is, brothers and sisters, OK to be there. Whenever you eat and drink you proclaim the Lord's death until He comes!

You come with empty hands to Jesus, our Passover lamb, knowing that death has passed over you, you have been delivered from slavery ... but you come looking for that Promised land. A meal of peace, and a meal of longing.

What kind of relationship does God want with us? What did he give His body and blood to achieve? In the book of Revelation Jesus says, 'I stand at the door and knock. If anyone hears my voice and opens the door, I will come in and eat with that person, and they with me.' God invites you to a meal where He gives you His very self. May our eyes be opened to the mystery of the cross, and our hearts respond to His invitation.

The Narrative of The Cross

Gethsemane and Calling

Matthew 26:36-46
Derek Walmsley. 29th April 2018

THE READING and CONTEXT
> 'Then Jesus went with his disciples to a place called
> Gethsemane, and he said to them, "Sit here while I go over
> there and pray."' (Matthew 26:36)

My wife and I were in Gethsemane 11 years ago when I was on
sabbatical.
In Gethsemane (of all the places we went) – we and many others
were overcome with emotion. We sang 'How Deep the Father's
Love for Us' – unplanned and spontaneous.

IT was TOUGH for JESUS
It was really hard for Jesus! He was God but it was as tough as
anything could ever be. As CS Lewis said in Mere Christianity
> If I am drowning in a rapid river, a man who still has one
> foot on the bank may give me a hand which saves my life.
> Ought I to shout back (between my gasps) "No, it's not fair!
> You have an advantage! You're keeping one foot on the
> bank"? That advantage—call it "unfair" if you like—is the
> only reason why he can be of any use to me. To what will
> you look for help if you will not look to that which is
> stronger than yourself? Such is my own way of looking at
> what Christians call the Atonement.

But Jesus really really suffered.

This is where the victory over Satan was won. Jesus resisted the
temptation to give up or compromise. He was fully God and fully

human, and the human pain that lay ahead was too much to bear (almost).
In the parallel passage in Luke, Jesus's sweat is like drops of blood

THE MEANING of THE ATONEMENT
Currently popular in some circles to dismiss the idea of atonement as horrible concept – some even have described it as cosmic child abuse.
Let's be clear: The atonement was not a wrathful Father punishing his reluctant son in anger. Certainly not an angry God who feels better after someone has suffered some kind of revenge. When the Bible says 'vengeance is mine, says the Lord' it is describing God's perfect justice in dealing with sin.

God's wrath is justified. God loved us from before creation but our sin cannot be neglected. It is like the anger we feel about injustice – e.g. murder, Windrush etc. 'Something must be done'. But the line between good and bad runs through every human heart. We all merit 'wrath' to some degree.

I deserved my speeding fine for 'only' doing 35mph in 30mph zone.

WHAT GOD DID
At the cross, the Trinity were working together deal with our problem of sin *together*.

ABRAHAM AND ISAAC 'went on together' after Isaac asked about the sacrifice
> 'Abraham answered, "God himself will provide the lamb for the burnt offering, my son." And the two of them went on together.' (Genesis 22:8)

Beautifully ambiguous! But remember that Abraham is over 100 and Isaac is a teenager, so he could probably outrun his dad!

THE ACTION!

In our Bible reading, Jesus is with all the eleven in the garden after the Last Supper. He takes the inner group of three Peter, James, and John further into the garden. Then he goes further still to pray.

Note this:

> 'Then he returned to his disciples and found them sleeping. "Couldn't you men keep watch with me for one hour?" he asked Peter. "Watch and pray so that you will not fall into temptation. The spirit is willing, but the flesh is weak."' (Matthew 26:40)

THE WRONG MEANING

The danger here is that I preach a sermon about gritting our teeth and being like Jesus in battling through the pain. I could add to that something about 'not being like the disciples' – who 'failed'. But that would be to miss the whole point of the event and why it's recorded for us.

The lesson is not: – so you should watch and learn from the disciples' mistake and failure.

The RIGHT MEANING

Notice this bit:

> The spirit is willing, but the flesh is weak (v41)

You want to serve God but you struggle to do so, and

> 43 When he came back, he again found them sleeping, because their eyes were heavy. 44 So he left them and went away once more and prayed the third time, saying the same thing. (v43-44)

Did you notice? He does not berate them anymore. In fact he didn't really berate them the first time. He was sad for them not angry with them. It seems at first that when he asks them to watch with him, he's asking them to look out for trouble. But it seems that he's concerned for their safety above his agony.

'Watch & pray so you don't fall into temptation'

And the third time he lets them sleep on!

SO WHAT DOES THIS MEAN FOR US?

What we can learn is that we all fail and yet Jesus still dies for us.
He anticipates our struggles, but 'God demonstrates his love for
us in that while we were still sinners Christ died for us.'
Our calling is therefore to respond to God's great love – not to
appease him but to please him.

I will not boast in anything,
No gifts, no power, no wisdom;
But I will boast in Jesus Christ,
His death and resurrection.

The Narrative of The Cross

Failure is not Final: Peter's Betrayal

Matthew 26:17-30, Luke 22:31-35
Dan Watts. 22nd April 2018

'Success is not final, failure is not fatal: it is the courage to continue that counts.' Winston Churchill

Sooner or later, everyone will experience failure. There are some people here today who have had more successes than failures, but failure is a universal experience. Some of the greatest people in history have had their life checkered with failure. Vincent van Gogh only sold one painting while he was alive. Albert Einstein failed his math exam. Walt Disney was fired because of a lack of creativity only to become the greatest graphic artist in history. Michel Jordan failed to make his high school basketball team.

Some of the greatest figures throughout Scripture have experienced failure. God promised Abraham a son with his wife Sarah but after two decades they couldn't wait and he impregnated his wife's servant. Moses was a murderer and became a fugitive before he became God's chosen instrument to free his people from slavery. God made King David committed adultery and then had her husband killed. And yet, he became a man after God's own heart. Saul was the greatest persecutor of the early church and murdered many followers of Jesus only to become its greatest missionary, evangelist, theologian and church planter.

Peter, the man whom Jesus called 'The Rock' and said, 'Upon you I will build my church' denied Jesus three times. Yet he becomes the leader of the disciples and the early church. Today we are looking at the story of an 'epic' failure – Peter's denial of Jesus. Whenever I read the gospels I am always struck by the humanity of Peter, the fact that he gets it so spectacularly wrong on so many occasions gives me encouragement. When I think of Peter I immediately think of 'foot IN mouth' disease. He so often seems to open his mouth before engaging his brain. He opens his mouth and climbs in with both feet. Peter says what he thinks and often acts without thinking.

Remember the time (Matt 14) that he and the other disciples are in a boat in the middle of a storm on the sea of Galilee. Jesus appears and they think it's a ghost until he says 'it is I'. Peter immediately says *'tell me to come to you on the water'*. He speaks and acts without thinking, he jumps out of the boat and starts walking on water before gradually sinking and almost drowning.

Or the time that Jesus was explaining to his disciples that he must go to Jerusalem, suffer at the hands of religious leaders, be killed and then raised to life on the third day (Matt 17). Peter jumps in with his response *'never, Lord'*, 'This shall never happen to you'. Peter doesn't get Jesus' mission and the purpose of his life – his impetuous response reveals his misunderstanding. Jesus replies by calling Peter Satan – *'Get behind me, Satan!'*. Seems pretty harsh, but 6 verses earlier he was the first disciple to respond to Jesus question 'who do you say I am' with the response *'you are the Christ, the Son of the Living God'*.

How about the time that Jesus, Peter and John go up the mountain (Matt 9). A cloud descends and Jesus is transfigured before them and then Moses and Elijah appear. Peter says shall I build three shelters so we can camp over. I suspect it is a kind of nervous response. The glory of God is being revealed in a bright shining light then Moses and Elijah appear. My guess is that Peter is feeling rather anxious and afraid – so he says the first thing that pops into his head *'shall I build three shelters'*.
Or the time they are in Gethsemane praying after the Passover meal and the soldiers come to arrest Jesus (John 18). Peter lashes out with his sword and lops off the ear of the High Priests servant. Jesus heals the man and is then led away.

We get the picture of a man who was passionate, courageous, adventurous, willing to take a risk. He was bullish, always ready to take a lead and make the big gesture. He was the leader of the rest of the twelve, always speaking first. With this kind of personality, he had some amazing moments and some 'epic fails'.

In today's reading Jesus has finished the Passover meal with his disciples and in front of the rest of the disciples Jesus warns Peter of some serious Satanic attack coming his way. Jesus told Peter that he was going to fail. '*When you have turned again*,' meant, 'When you've come to your senses and realize that you've failed, you must turn to your brothers. I'm going to pray for you.' Jesus knows that Peter will deny him and fail, but he also know that he will return from his failure. Jesus knows that we too will fail and he his praying for our return.

Imagine if Jesus said you were going to deny Him in front of everyone you knew. Peter responded in the same way we probably would. He began to defend himself, '*Lord, I am ready to go with you both to prison and to death.' (Luke 22:33)* Peter told Jesus he wouldn't fail Him, he was more loyal and faithful than Jesus knew. He would follow Him even to death. Peter is adamant. Never will he deny Jesus. Peter, big, bombastic, bull-in-a-china-shop Peter, vows to be the rock Jesus wanted him to be. Dependable. Steady. Strong. Even if he has to die, he promises, nothing will come between him and his Lord. Everyone else may fail, but not Peter. *Don't worry,* he assures Jesus, *I got this.*

Jesus replies, 'I tell you, Peter, the rooster will not crow this day, until you deny three times that you know me.' (Luke 22:34) Jesus explained He knew what He was talking about, Peter would deny the fact he even knew Him. It wasn't going to be in some distant future, but within the next twelve hours. All the bravado and faith Peter claimed to have would be for nothing; he would deny Jesus three times. He wasn't just going to talk bad about Him, but rather completely deny he even knew Him. Jesus told Peter this then ended the conversation and moved on. A couple hours later, Peter denied him three times.

As the High Priest was trying Jesus, Peter stayed faithful and was there with other onlookers who were curious to see what was going to happen to this guy named Jesus who claimed to be the Messiah. People begin to realise that Peter knew Jesus. They recognised his accent and claimed he was a friend of His. Twice, Peter denied it and told them they had the wrong guy.

*'But Peter said, "Man, I do not know what you are talking about."
And immediately, while he was still speaking, the rooster crowed.
And the Lord turned and looked at Peter. And Peter remembered
the saying of the Lord, how he had said to him, "Before the rooster
crows today, you will deny me three times." And he went out and
wept bitterly.' (Luke 22:60-62)*

As he was speaking the words of denial, a rooster crowed in the background. The rooster crowing didn't set off Peter's realisation of what he'd done. He probably didn't even hear it. But somehow, in the midst of the chaos of the moment, Peter and Jesus locked eyes; Peter's fear and anger dissipated and he realised that all Jesus had said came true. He realised what he had done, was filled with shame and guilt and ran away weeping bitterly

Use your imagination, how do you think Peter felt? Jesus turned and looked at Peter, Jesus did not look at Peter in anger, Jesus did not look at Peter in disappointment. Scripture does not tell us how Jesus looked at Peter. But, with what we know of Jesus, we can guess that He looked at Peter with love. Peter may have seen that look and realised that Jesus still loved him.
What do you think Peter felt? Well, how would you feel, what would you feel? Peter had vehemently denied that he would stumble because of his association with Christ. He had said that he would suffer prison or even death for Jesus sake and now, he denied that he knew Him. Did Peter feel shame? Perhaps disgust

at himself, remorse or guilt?

This is an epic failure. This is Peter who said, *'To whom shall we go, You and You alone have the words of eternal life.'* Who said, *'You are the Christ, the Son of the living God.'* This is Peter, the great leader, the great preacher. How can this happen? This is a believer. And this is not just a momentary slip-up. His denials are strung out over two hours and the first one was a shock and a surprise, but the next two were pre-meditated responses, not just knee-jerk. The text is brief but the experience was strung out over those two hours. In fact, the same two hours that Jesus is on trial before Annas and Caiaphas. Jesus on trial for two hours from one to three, Peter's denial from one to three, they run concurrently. Christ is seen in glorious triumphant, speaking honestly knowing it will cost Him His life. Peter speaks dishonestly trying to preserve his life.

In the first century Middle Eastern culture, if someone broke his or her word three times, it would be appropriate for you to break relationship permanently with that person. Peter knows he has blown it, big time with Jesus. His best friend, his master has the right to break relationship with him – for ever, no way back.

Where did Peter go after he denied Christ? The answer is, we don't know for certain because the Bible doesn't say. But we can guess that Peter did what most of us do when we have blown it. When we have made a huge mistake, the last thing we want is to be around other people, especially the ones who know us best and love us the most. Having let them down, we don't want to see them at all. *Sin separates us from God and from God's people.* Sin isolates us so that the devil can convince that, having made such a stupid mistake, no one wants to be around us again, ever. So we spend our hours in a miserable prison of self-imposed solitary confinement.

I think that's what happened to Peter that weekend. Wherever he was, he must have felt alone in the world. The last thing we are told is that after Jesus looked at him, Peter wept bitterly. We are not told where Peter was during the crucifixion on Friday or during the burial late that afternoon. We can guess that he retreated to some lonely spot, there to replay those awful moments in his mind so he could beat himself up all over again and ask, 'Why? Why did I do it? What made me think I was so much better than the others? How could I have been so stupid?' and 'What does Jesus think of me now?'

We find an answer to that last question in the fact that Jesus made a special appearance to Peter sometime on Easter Sunday. We don't know where or when precisely nor do we know how long the meeting lasted. But twice the New Testament mentions that the meeting took place: *'It is true! The Lord has risen and has appeared to Simon' (Luke 24:34).* And in 1 Corinthians 15:4-5. *'He was raised on the third day according to the Scriptures, and that he appeared to Peter, and then to the Twelve'.*

What amazing grace. There will be no public humiliation. Since Peter denied Christ, things must first be settled between the two of them. With wisdom and grace, Christ comes after Peter and doesn't wait for him to make the first move. Failure is not final because failure is an event not an identity. You are not defined by what you have done in the past or present. Jesus is full of mercy and grace. He is ready to forgive, praying for your return.

We see in the life of Peter that failure is not final. We know that Peter denied Jesus; it could have been the end of the friendship. But in John 21 Jesus meets Peter over breakfast after he and his friends have been fishing on Galilee. Jesus reinstates and reaffirms Peter as his friend and he goes on to be a preacher, church planter and church leader.

In the cross we see that what looked like a failure – the death of Jesus, the one who had come to bring about a new Kingdom rule, die at the hands of the Roman oppressors. Was it in fact not the end of the story? Three days later Jesus was raised to life again. Failure, or what looks like failure is not final.

Failure is not final, we see it in Peter, we see it in the cross, we see it in our own lives.

The Narrative of The Cross

'The Kiss of Betrayal'

Matthew 26:47-50
Laura Brett. 6th May 2018

The story has often been told of Mr. H. St. John standing in the private chapel of Keble College, Oxford, contemplating Holman Hunt's masterpiece, 'The Light of the World'. Suddenly, the silence was broken by a crowd of tourists led by a guide, a man with a particularly strident voice. After a hasty explanation of the painting, he announced, 'The original of this picture was sold for £5,000.' Without a moment's hesitation Mr. St. John stepped forward and said very quietly, 'Ladies and gentlemen, may I say that the true Original of this picture was sold for thirty pieces of silver?' After a moment's silence, the crowd of people passed out of the chapel without another word...

Betrayal... being stabbed in the back by those that you trust... deception and lies... it all hurts, doesn't it? The wounds run deep.

I'd imagine that if I asked you to raise your hands – each and every one of us could remember a time, or perhaps be currently struggling in the fight with a situation which has left us feeling betrayed, hurt, let down, vulnerable and disappointed.

It is the experience of living in this world... and sadly very few of us escape unscathed.

When I think of a kiss – I think of intimacy and love – it's an outward symbol, an act of beauty – it represents that we care and are concerned for that other person, and in the Middle East where these events took place, it was and still is widely common to greet friends, colleagues, masters and family with a kiss.

And yet, this kiss of Judas upon Jesus' face is anything but a mark of love, respect and honour. It became the ultimate act of betrayal in the whole of history – an act which prompted Jesus' arrest by the Chief Priests and Elders and subsequent trial... and we're going to unpack that a little further today.

Someone once said '(that sin) is never so horrible as when it uses holy things to accomplish evil purposes'. Earlier in Luke 22:3 during The Passover we read: 'then Satan entered Judas, called Iscariot, one of the Twelve' – and it was at this moment that Judas went to the chief priests and officers of the temple guard and discussed with them how he might betray Jesus.

It is at this point that we are catapulted into the mystery of Predestination (the thought that God has planned everything in advance) versus Free Will – this is something that the Scriptures holds tightly in tension and it is not something I am going to try and discuss today... Nevertheless, we can learn so much from this act of human betrayal and it can teach about the failings of our own human nature and selfish ambitions, and yet how God still loves us and He still reaches out for us through his ceaseless grace and mercy.

Just recently I watched the movie 'Mary Magdalene' at the cinema and I was completely blown away. It was a beautiful, captivating, gentle and perfectly-paced depiction of the Rabbi they called Jesus of Nazareth, through the eyes of a flawed, but totally forgiven and restored young woman. And yet God chose her to be the Apostle of Apostles – she was present at the crucifixion and the resurrection – she was the first to announce to the other disciples 'I have seen the Lord'. And as a flawed, but forgiven young (ish!) woman – that gives me eternal hope!

But I was also deeply moved at how I began to see the person of Judas through a completely different lens. It was like God scraped those 5-year old Sunday School scales right from my eyes of 'Oh yeah, Judas – he's just the bad guy in the story'! and instead replaced them with a pair of 'spiritual glasses' and I began to see him quite differently!

I think it's really easy for us to criticise Judas – but how do we shape up?

We can too often overlook the fact that Judas was chosen by Jesus to be one of his twelve disciples. The only non-Galilean, actually. Over a three-year period of time, Judas had the privilege of enjoying close fellowship with Jesus and he had been richly blessed to be in the company of the Rabbi and His other disciples. He chose him. Just like he chooses us today. Ephesians Chapter 1 'For he chose us in him before the creation of the world to be holy and blameless in in his sight'. And so Jesus loved Judas, just as he loves us. But despite being quite literally so close to the Saviour – he'd seen him walk on water, heal the sick and raise the dead, eaten with him, debated with him, prayed with him – in fact, he couldn't have been much closer physically – spiritually... he was so far away.

I think it's also easy to forget that it wasn't just Judas who betrayed him. It says in verse 56 'Then all the disciples deserted him and fled' – they cut and run! – you see, the disciples all shared a persistent misunderstanding of Jesus' mission. No matter how hard they tried, they often just didn't get it. I guess that's a bit like us too sometimes...

The trouble with Judas is that he was greedy. He allowed his own desires to place him in a position where Satan could manipulate him. In the Mary Magdalene movie, Judas is portrayed as a larger than life, excitable puppy – often speaking before thinking, a little socially awkward, impatient – perhaps struggling somewhat with his own mental wellbeing... Judas was just desperate to see this Kingdom of God that was being spoken about come NOW! and, therefore, he left himself wide open to manipulating the situation for his own motives...

But whatever your own feelings towards Judas – in betraying Jesus, he made the greatest mistake in history and we today can learn from his mistake...

So, firstly, be on your guard! Do not let the devil get even a foothold! Evil plans and motives can leave us completely open to being used by Satan for an even greater evil. The consequences of these deeds can be so devastating that even small lies and little wrongdoings have serious results.

The minor argument that a couple have never settled could lead to a lack of communication and consequential relationship breakdown, which could lead to an affair, to a divorce and so much pain and hurt...

The slight compromise in your financial integrity, later becomes a major tax dodge and a possible criminal offence...

A few unkind words or gossip said in private about a good friend could eventually lead to division, character defamation, hatred and unforgiveness...
That quick look of lust at someone other than your partner might lead to trawling the internet in the dark of night for pornographic images...

Or simply making your life so busy with stuff and your work so important that it pushes the most important things away - and what once was a healthy daily prayer life has now become a squeezed weekly activity or even a dormant exercise...

And I could go on and on...

We pray, don't we 'Lead us not into temptation... but deliver us from evil'.

It makes me think of Edmund's betrayal in C. S. Lewis' The Lion the Witch and The Wardrobe – what began as the tempting gift by The White Witch with some seemingly innocent Turkish Delight, turned out to be something far more sinister... deception, lies and betrayal. So 'Be on your guard! Stand firm in the faith. Be courageous and be strong' (1 Corinthians 16:3). 'Remember the devil prowls around like a roaring lion looking for someone to devour' (1 Peter 5:8).

So resist the devil – his lies, temptations and murmurings – and submit and align yourself with God...

Secondly, does your external presentation match your internal perspective?
You see on the surface, Judas' kiss of betrayal appeared to be an act of beauty, but from within we know that it was motivated by greed and personal gain. And the truth is that any time we put greater value on other things than on the Lord – we too are committing the Kiss of Betrayal.

Jesus knew that he was about to be betrayed by one of his closest friends. Earlier in Luke Chapter 22 Jesus says 'The Son of Man will go as it has been decreed, but woe to the man who betrays him'.

Although Judas was chosen – he, like us, was not immune from temptation. This is the paradox – although it had been said, declared in scripture, evil had been allowed to enter him and by his own free will, he consented to betray Jesus. Predestination does not supplant our own responsibility to choose.

So how might we betray Jesus with a kiss today? Is what we are displaying on the outside, matching up to our hearts on the inside? Do we give our money away lavishly because it is an overflow of our hearts and for what God has done for us in His great mercy – or do we give it away begrudgingly so that we can talk about it, feel good about ourselves and take all the praise...

Do we come into his House today, pour out our hearts to the Lord in praise and worship.... and then go home and bad mouth our neighbour, or walk by on the other side from somebody in need, or fail to turn to him first when we know that we should...what about when we let him down by what we've done, or said or thought? Each time, it's just like another kiss of betrayal...

But you know there is no escape! It says in 1 Samuel 16:7 'People look at the outward appearance, but the LORD looks at the heart'. The Lord knows. Nothing is hidden from him. Psalm 139 v 15 'Nothing about me is hidden from you!' . You see, He knew Judas was going to betray him and he knows your heart and my heart too.... so we need to stop trying to hide it. And simply just come to him with open hearts and open minds... and let Him do a work in us.

So firstly, be on your guard! Do not let the devil get even a foothold!, secondly, make sure that your external presentation matches up with your internal perspective... and finally...

God's plan and his purposes are worked out even in the worst possible events...

Whatever his plan, at some point Judas realised that he'd messed up and he tried to undo the evil he had done by returning the money to the priests, but it was too late. The wheels of God's most sovereign plan had been set in motion...

How sad that Judas ended his life in despair without experiencing the gift of forgiveness and reconciliation which God gives us freely through his son Jesus Christ. We are fortunate to live with the benefit of hindsight – we know the end of the story. But Judas was riddled with failure, guilt and shame - he had spectacularly let down his beloved teacher, master and friend and had been solely responsible for his arrest. His eyes were completely blinded to the truth - he realised the gravity of his mistake – but for Judas, it was too late.

Albert Einstein once said 'Failure is success in progress' – I guess we could argue that Judas and his apparent failings paved the way for God's salvation plan for the world – and I often wonder if God in His great mercy welcomed Judas with open arms into His Kingdom. Judas - the one who sent Jesus to his death, to give us our salvation through his resurrection. A bittersweet part of Redemption's Story – there was never a Plan B – Jesus was always the Plan.

When Jesus died on the cross he brought man and God together again in beautiful fellowship with one another. The curtain was torn from top to bottom. He carried all of our sin, anything we have done or will ever do on the weight of that heavy cross and when he died – it all died too, once and for all.

And we now have this great privilege where we can come to the Father through Him. What a wonderful end to that story that only God could have written!

So thank you Judas. Thank you that we can think again about our commitment to God and the presence of His Holy Spirit within us.

And so my question to us all:

Do you want to choose despair and death like Judas and betray Jesus with a kiss?

Or do you want to choose repentance, forgiveness, hope and eternal life through God's free gift to us all.

Father God, thank you that you love us in spite of our sins, and that your son Jesus Christ came to suffer and die on the cross to pay for them. Today, we come simply as we are and we say sorry for the times when we have lived a life of betrayal and hypocrisy. Let us honestly acknowledge our acts of betrayal... Father God cleanse our hearts we pray and help each and every one of us to receive the friendship Jesus offers us through His forgiveness and redeeming grace. Amen.

The Narrative of The Cross

Challenging the myth of Redemptive Violence

Matthew 26:51-56

Guy Donegan-Cross. 6th May 2018

This is a dark hour. The world can be violent, difficult, scary and full of betrayal. Sometimes that's in the barrage of war stories that come at us. Sometimes in the conflicts we face. Here we see Jesus in the eye of a storm. Betrayer's kiss, swords, clubs, a mob, darkness, arrest, fighting. God in chains. Yet...so calm, so tough in loving, so in control. How? What gave Jesus the strength to not fight as the world fights? To not rely on the power of the sword?

This is vitally important, because how we respond to our enemies, or conflicts, or darkness is what defines us as Christians. It's our distinguishing mark. Everyone can be nice to their friends, but it's the ability to treat your enemies with love that makes Christ-followers different. Bless those who persecute you. Really? How? And this is not an abstract question either. Because if you ever stand up for Christ, for self-giving love, for God's kingdom, you will confront, or be confronted by darkness. When it comes, whether through your TV screen, or the person next door who doesn't warm to you, how will you and I be tough enough to love? Like Jesus, at this moment?

This can play out at a very personal level. I was talking to someone in our church who is experiencing a real sense of alienation in the workplace. Not being included in a party invitation. Being left out of the loop in some key decisions. Emails go back and forth, but relationships can become strained. The amount of time to process things is never there, and you can feel increasingly insecure or wounded. Perhaps slightly betrayed by a friend. Or surrounded by people who want to shut you up. The temptation is to pick up a sword and lash out.

It can also play out at a global level. We see threats coming at us every day. Rogue nations. Terrorist attacks. Hate speech. Again, the temptation is to lash out, self-protect, get them before they get you. Few have the imagination for peace, for bridge-building.

Whether or not you would call yourself a pacifist, and we don't have time to explore that fully, I think most Christians would agree that even if you can't go all the way in being a pacifist, you should attempt to get 95% of the way there. The problem is, we are given very few stories or precious little guidance by our culture from day one of our lives as to what this would look like. The way we are discipled by stories, films and news narratives would far more likely having us reaching for the sword like Peter than refusing to engage in the battle like Jesus.

Whether we like it or not, for example, our instincts are shaped so much by stories that work like this. There is a hero. There is a bad guy. The bad guy does a terrible thing. It all looks hopeless. But then, the hero tools up. Our adrenaline starts pumping at this point. I remember a classic scene in the film 'The Matrix', for example, when the central character inhabits this generated world, and says the immortal line, 'We need guns, lots of guns.' Boom! Suddenly, we are surrounded by thousands of them. They look so cool. He selects a few and tucks them into his belt. Now we know he is going to win.

That's how the world thinks, by and large. And whether it's in our workplace, or in global affairs, we are hugely affected by it. Sociologists call, it 'The myth of redemptive violence.' The deeply ingrained story in our souls that it is possible to win by lashing out with the bigger sword, gun, or insult. It is ultimately driven by fear. A fear which says, 'Get them, before they get you.' Because that will ultimately sort everything out.
But at his arrest... Jesus goes the opposite way. He doesn't hit back. He doesn't resist. He doesn't defend himself. He is honest about confronting hypocrisy – why didn't you arrest me earlier?

– but he allows evil to have the upper hand at the expense of his own safety. He loves his enemies. Calls his betrayer, 'Friend'. It's very impractical. Stupid, even, according to our world.

The difference between the way of Jesus, and the way of the world is this: He doesn't follow the myth of redemptive violence; He rests on the truth of unseen but redemptive love. It's the hardest path. It's tough to love, far tougher than hitting back. To say no to violence, and yes to peace is much, much more difficult. Who is the bravest in this story? The one armed with a sword, or a club? Or the one who refuses to hit back? You have to be tough to take the initiative in building a bridge to the colleague who has hurt you, rather than putting your energy into defending yourself. You have to be really strong to lay down your life for your enemies.

In a broken world, what's the source of being able to stay calm like Christ, not to lash out, not to meet aggression with aggression? For Jesus, it was simple. He entrusted himself to His Father. People saw swords and clubs. He saw the presence of His Father, who could send legions of angels. People saw a story of force being the way to win. Jesus knew that violence always begets violence – if you defeat your enemy you invariably push the battle on to the next generation – and He saw a bigger picture. One in which giving up His own life was the best way to win. His Father was in control. His life was not His own. What could these people really do to Him? They could only kill His body, not take His soul. Rather than being driven by fear, he entrusts himself to the one who is ultimately in control. His Father.

George Muller found the secret of setting aside self for Christ and gave this testimony: 'There was a day wherein I died, utterly died to George Muller and his opinions, preferences, tastes and will; died to the world, its approval or censure; died to the approval of blame of even my brethren and friends; and since then I have studied only to show myself approved unto God.'

If you are in the eye of the storm, tempted to defend yourself rather than to build bridges. Or tempted to indulge in simplistic knee-jerk politics instead of the tough path of seeking peace towards others, then we are Peter wildly lashing out, rather than Jesus who looks to His Father in all things. We must give up two illusions: one: the false idea that we can control others. And two: the idea that greater strength is the means to defeat your opponents. You may be able to contain them for a while, you may be able to shut that annoying person up with your witty put down, or beat that enemy into submission, but they as long as they remain your enemy you will still be in darkness together.

For my friend struggling at work the simple question is this: can you entrust yourself to Jesus, who is Lord? Because in the same way that Jesus entrusted Himself to His Father, and therefore had peace in the storm, so, too, if you know that Jesus is Lord over you in your workplace, only that knowledge will transform the situation. If Jesus is your Lord, you can trust Him for justice – He knows the full picture. If Jesus is Lord, then there is nothing that can ultimately harm you. And if Jesus is your Lord, then he is also Lord over the person you find challenging, and wants to meet them too.

People who can respond to aggression with love because Jesus is their Lord have a wonderful opportunity to do two things. Once the missionary to China Hudson Taylor was standing by a riverbank, dressed as a poor Chinese person. He hailed a boat to take him across the river. Just as the boat was drawing near, a wealthy Chinese man came along who did not recognise Hudson Taylor as a foreigner because he had dressed like the Chinese. So when the boat came the wealthy Chinese man pushed Taylor aside with such force that the latter fell into the mud. Hudson Taylor, however, said nothing; but the boatman refused to take his fellow-countryman, saying, 'No, that foreigner called me, and the boat is his, he must go first.' The Chinese traveller was amazed and astounded when he realised he had blundered.

Hudson Taylor did not complain. He didn't return like for like. Instead, he invited the man into the boat with him and began to tell him what it was in him that made him behave in such a manner. It was the love of Christ that compelled him.

The first thing those who do not fight back can do is start to bear witness to the precious love of Christ through their refusal to engage. It is our opportunity to put His love on display.

And secondly, let's go back to the Matrix. The central character reaches a point towards the end when he realises that he is living in a generated world where everything is illusion. The bullets coming at him, the enemies confronting him, have no real or lasting impact. And in a final scene, as a hail of bullets are coming towards him, rather than fighting back, he simply puts out his hand and says, 'No.' The bullets stop mid air. He takes hold of one and looks at it curiously. As he sees things for what they really are, the bullets fall to the floor, and the whole construct starts to fall to pieces.

In the garden, Jesus refused to play along with the myth of redemptive violence. He said no to replying with hatred, and because He knew His Father was in control, He said Yes to the path of costly, sin-bearing love.

What do you need to say, 'No' to? Hating your enemies? Fear of world events? The temptation to despise your colleagues because they don't treat you well?

If Jesus is Lord, you can entrust yourself to Him without fear.

If Jesus is Lord, you can meet anger with love.

If Jesus is Lord, you can start to play your part in a world which will be built on hope, not self-protection.

If Jesus is Lord, you can know that whatever your circumstances and trials, your future is secure. For the joy that was set before Him he endured the cross.

May we imitate and bear witness to the love that conquers all darkness.

The Narrative of The Cross

Jesus before Pilate

Luke 23:1-25
Bishop Helen-Ann Hartley. 13th May 2018

*'We believe in one God, the Father, the Almighty, maker of heaven
and earth, of all that is, seen and unseen...For our sake he was
crucified under Pontius Pilate, he suffered death and was buried...'*

I have said the Creed countless times. It contains in summary
form the essential tenets of the Christian faith. Two people from
Jesus' life story are mentioned: his mother Mary, and Pontius
Pilate. Given the relative amount of time that Jesus spent with
each, it is quite astonishing that Pilate should be immortalised in
this way, and yet, he is; Jesus' death and crucifixion are grounded
in a time and place, and Pilate plays a major part in this moment
in history.

I want you to imagine for a moment, that Pilate is appearing on
TV's *Mastermind*:

Name: Pontius Pilate;
Occupation: 5th prefect of the Roman province of Judaea, serving
under the Emperor Tiberius from the year 26 to 36;
Specialised subject: the trial and crucifixion of Jesus of Nazareth,
'King of the Jews' (alleged).

Pilate: A man of long-standing service to the Roman Empire; a
man of firm authority. Weak? Open to manipulation? Or
complex, flawed, and deeply human? Before we judge, if we were
in Pilate's sandals, how would we behave?

*'The very air that Pilate breathes, the voice
With which he speaks in judgment, all his powers*

Of perception and discrimination, choice,
Decision, all his years, his days and hours,
His consciousness of self, his every sense,
Are given by this prisoner, freely given.
The man who stands there making no defence,
Is God. His hands are tied, His heart is open.
And he bears Pilate's heart in his and feels
That crushing weight of wasted life. He lifts
It up in silent love. He lifts and heals.
He gives himself again with all his gifts
Into our hands. As Pilate turns away
A door swings open. This is judgment day.'

These words of the poet and priest Malcolm Guite evoke something of the weight of atmosphere that surrounds this episode in Luke's version of Jesus' journey to crucifixion. The encounter between Jesus and Pilate.

Helen Bond, a New Testament scholar at the University of Edinburgh has researched Pilate's life extensively (particularly in her 1998 book *Pontius Pilate in History and Interpretation*, Cambridge University Press). She reports that nothing is really known about Pilate until he arrives in Judaea in the year 26 in the first century. He was probably an Italian nobleman who rose to prominence through military service. There is an inscription found in Caeasarea Maritima in 1961 which gives Pilate the title *praefectus*, or prefect, a military term which tells us that Judaea had not long been under direct Roman rule, and that Pilate's chief job would have been to maintain law and order. Judaea was an outpost of the Roman Empire, and Pilate would only have had small army of soldiers at his disposal. But extensive research into first century history has shown us that Judaea in the first century was a hot-bed of social and political unrest. There were simmering tensions between the ruling elite and the ordinary people (which eventually resulted in a revolt against Roman rule from the 66 until the destruction of the Temple in 70); all of that forms something of the backdrop to the life of Jesus, and the immediate context that led to his death.

Religion and politics formed a heady mix in the first century, so while to some Jesus was a political threat, to others his challenge to the religious status quo made him a dangerous individual. Helen Bond writes: 'in ancient societies, the divide between "religion" and "politics" was not nearly so clear as it appears to most people in the western industrialised world. Religion permeated all aspects of people's lives, from private, individual decisions up to local and national government. Readers should not be surprised then to find a high priest listed alongside Herodian kings and Roman governors as part of the political landscape of first century Israel. These different rulers, in varying combinations, directed political life at the time of Jesus.'

The trial of Jesus before Pilate occurs in all four Gospels, and there are similarities and differences between the versions, cause largely by different sources that the evangelists used, and their need to edit the material to make sense to their audience. It is certain however, that the Gospel of Mark (the earliest Gospel), was Luke's main source. Luke's account significantly places stress on Pilate's reluctance to act against Jesus. Instead, the weight is placed on Jewish determination to have Jesus condemned to death, or rather, the determination on the part of some Jews, for this clearly was a matter of internal debate within Judaism; we aren't dealing with a straight-forward scenario of Jews against Jesus, Judaism was far more varied in the first century than we sometimes presume.

Luke invites us to look at Jesus for who he is (utterly lacking in power yet utterly full of power), to puzzle about Pilate's state of mind; to wonder why Herod becomes involved, and finally to face the temptation of another saviour from the point of view of the crowd: a man called Barabbas. The scene is tense and chaotic – we are in the midst of the crowd, what would we do, and who would we choose if we were there? Jesus, Barabbas? We are meant to push ourselves perilously close to choosing Barabbas; that's the point.

While we consider those questions, Luke does something interesting with the narrative. Luke alone introduces an appearance before Herod Antipas (the son of Herod the Great, who was king when Jesus was born), something which historians have wondered about. It would be possible, some commentators have suggested to imagine that Roman justice would allow a person to be tried in the place where they lived, but the handing over responsibility for this to a non-Roman would be very unusual. It is thought that this apparently obscure episode may well be the influence of Psalm 2.1-2 which is quoted in Acts 4.25-26 (Psalm 2:1-2 says this: 'Why do the nations conspire, and the peoples plot in vain? The kings of the earth set themselves, and the rulers take counsel together, against the LORD and his anointed...'). The weight of the two leaders conspiring together (Pilate and Herod) seems to imply that both had something to gain from the episode? Both were politicians who had to play games not just to remain in power, but perhaps to avoid their own demise in the face of Roman rule which could at times be dangerously unstable and open to extreme violence. Whatever the explanation, Luke presents Herod as someone who has been perplexed by Jesus, and then joins in the mocking of him. If you have seen or heard Andrew Lloyd Webber's *Jesus Christ Superstar*, you may remember the lyrics of this song by Herod to Jesus:

Jesus, I am overjoyed to meet you face to face.
You've been getting quite a name all around the place.
Healing cripples, raising from the dead.
And now I understand you're God,
At least, that's what you've said....
Come on, King of the Jews.
I only ask what I'd ask any superstar.
What is it that you have got that puts you where you are.
I am waiting, yes I'm a captive fan.

The New Testament scholar Tom Wright asks us to imagine the scene between Jesus and Herod as being rather like that of James Bond meeting the villain, 'we meet at last, Mr Bond.' How easy is to turn from perplexed curiosity to hate and rejection. Herod fulfils that role in this passage, heightening the tension and the anticipation of what will happen to Jesus. Whatever it means, what is clear is that Luke tells us that Herod and Pilate became friends after that day. Two leaders bound together in the intoxicating grasp of power. It is deeply ironic that one of Luke's great themes in his Gospel is the expansion of the good news to the Gentiles; here at this crucial moment, that extension between Empire and Gentiles is presented in an ironic twist – both Pilate and Herod are Gentiles, or at least as good as Gentiles (Herod was an Idumaean, a non-Jew). Jesus brings about reconciliation despite what they have done to him. Not even condemnation to death can destroy the reconciling power of God.

It's important to understand this episode taken together with the interaction between Jesus and Pilate as part of Luke's intent to heighten why Jesus' power was unlike the power at work in his day – the power of politics and subversion; Jesus' power, God's power was a truth unlike that. Luke wants us to understand this, and so presents Jesus in absolute contrast to the men with whom he is now in conversation with. Three times Pilate declares Jesus innocent of the charges he has been accused of; Luke is keen to stress that Jesus was innocent of political insurrection, the issue was a religious one. Pilate goes along with it, yet in so doing, he unwittingly witnesses to the truth itself: that Jesus was the Messiah, the king of the Jews.

Without Pilate there would have been no crucifixion. Only Pilate had the authority to condemn Jesus to death. So we could suggest that he did what he needed to do, and in so doing, played his part in God's plan for salvation.

'The very air that Pilate breathes, the voice

With which he speaks in judgment, all his powers
Of perception and discrimination, choice,
Decision, all his years, his days and hours,
His consciousness of self, his every sense,
Are given by this prisoner, freely given.
The man who stands there making no defence,
Is God. His hands are tied, His heart is open.
And he bears Pilate's heart in his and feels
That crushing weight of wasted life. He lifts
It up in silent love. He lifts and heals.
He gives himself again with all his gifts
Into our hands. As Pilate turns away
A door swings open. This is judgment day.'

The Narrative of The Cross

'Do not weep for me.' Things that Knock you Sideways

Luke 23:26-31
Guy Donegan-Cross. 27th May 2018

Jesus being led to his execution...Simon of Cyrene out of nowhere being press-ganged...Jesus predicts the fall and slaughter of Jerusalem a few decades in the future...and yet says, 'Don't weep for me...' When the wood is green, he says, it will burn with less ferocity. When it is dry, the suffering will be even greater. Chaos, pain, suffering, evil...and in the middle of it, Jesus saying, 'Don't weep.' What? Take all this horror on the chin?

Before we get into this, a few comments of interest. Jesus is followed by daughters of Jerusalem, weeping for Him. Let's note that this is both an affirmation of the bravery, courage and significance of women in the Bible, and that for those who would want to land the blame for his death on Jewish people for anti-Semitic purposes, Luke is clearly showing that the crowd that originally cried, 'Crucify Him!' pretty quickly no longer wants to be complicit in his death. Simon of Cyrene – an African Jew from what's now Eastern Libya, likely to have travelled to Jerusalem for the Passover. What's interesting is that the historian Josephus confirms that there was a big community of Jews in Cyrene at that time. Final detail: Jesus is predicting the fall of Jerusalem in AD 70, and so tells the women that it would be better if they had not had children so they would not have to experience the grief of the loss of all their sons. A bitter kind of blessing not to have a child. He predicts an evil so calamitous that people will think they would be better off dead, with mountains falling on them to cover them.

Do you ever feel perplexed by the horror of the world? A horror so great that sometimes it would be better for some not to have been born? Great books and films often portray this at the heart of things. Joseph Conrad's 'Heart of Darkness' tells the story of a group sailing into the Congo delta – a metaphor for the twisted brokenness of life. 'We penetrated deeper and deeper into the heart of darkness' and at the centre of it they meet the mysterious Mr Kurtz whose pivotal lines are simply, 'The horror! The horror!' If you have ever seen the film, 'Apocalypse Now' which transposes it into Vietnam you see Marlon Brando doing the same thing, having talked about his admiration, moral will, and genius of people who could commit pure acts of evil. Do you have a faith, an understanding of the world, that can deal with this horror and face it? Jesus did.

It's quite common for people to say that the presence of evil in the world, of suffering, is a reason for not believing in the goodness of God. A philosopher called Cyril Joad put it plainly: 'I was for years baffled by the problem of pain and evil; in fact, it was this problem that for years denied belief in the Christian religion.'

So the presence of evil is a huge challenge. But I want to say why believing in a godless world makes the presence of evil and suffering even more of a challenge. Because paradoxically for the Christian, as we see Jesus confronting the reality of evil, I believe following Jesus can help us live in this world with realism and hope in a way that believing in a godless world can't.

I want to show why truly believing in a godless existence has nothing to offer in the face of evil, in contrast to the worldview of the Bible which not only explains it, but also provides the only eternal and realistic remedy to the horror.

When, as Jesus predicted, the Romans sacked Jerusalem, Josephus writes that, 'Round the Altar the heaps of corpses grew higher and higher, while down the Sanctuary steps poured a river of blood and the bodies of those killed at the top slithered to the bottom.' Ten thousand Jews had their throats cut within the Temple. It became hell on earth. Blessed were the women who had no sons. It is a picture of all the worst of human history. What could be said about this by those for whom God does not exist? There are many people who believe the world is godless but who live relatively good lives, by human standards probably better than you or I. I'm not arguing whether atheists can be good or not. If they can, good for them. But I am asking what have they really got to say about the reality of evil. Can they explain it?

Richard Dawkins says there is no god, and therefore there is, 'at bottom, no design, no purpose, no evil, no good, nothing but blind, pitiless indifference.' So one of the questions he therefore can't answer is why should anything be called good or evil anyway. Once he was asked in an interview, 'Ultimately, your belief that rape is wrong is as arbitrary as the fact that we've evolved five fingers rather than six.' To which Dawkins responded, 'You could say that, yeah.' Dostoevsky the novelist put it like this: 'If God does not exist, everything is permissible'. He wasn't saying that people can't be good. He's saying that the foundations of morality are removed. You can't call anything evil. It just is.

In 1924 two men, Leopold and Loeb, killed a young boy Robert Franks, who was walking home from a game. They disfigured his face so he couldn't be recognised, and sent a ransom note to his father saying he was still alive. They nearly got away with it – the police closed the case. But an investigative reporter revisited the scene, found a pair of glasses, traced the opticians, and found the two men. It was an infamous case. The amazing thing was that during the trial Leopold and Loeb showed no remorse, no concern for rights of boy, no motive. Why did they do it then? Simply - because they could. It was an experiment. They believed God is dead. There was therefore no divine moral code any more. They took the idea that human beings made their own rules to the extreme. Committing an act of pure evil as an act of will.

Is this really the way things are? I really hope not. Because generally speaking according to an experiment done in the 1960s two thirds of us are capable of ministering electric shocks to people beyond what they can bear as long as someone in a lab coat tells us to do it. We are scary!

We might find evil challenges faith, and the Bible's full of people saying, 'Where are you God?' but let's not pretend that without God there is anything to offer. In fact, name me the person who really, really lives as if there truly is no higher love or purpose. Who gets out of bed each morning as if there is no meaning other than to ensure the survival of the fittest?

So, in contrast, it's really important to know that Jesus knew about evil, he predicted it, and He lived within a world which was just as horrifying as anything we face. When I see the flagellated Jesus carrying his cross, his own body broken so much already that Simon of Cyrene had to carry it for Him, I see one for whom horror, pain, evil, selfishness and hypocrisy doesn't diminish or challenge His trust in His father. You don't see Jesus asking, 'If God is good, how can I be suffering? Why will these terrible things happen?'

In fact, no one ever asks that question in the New Testament. They were canny about things: the reality that there is good we have fallen away from – we call that sin. We are not just drifting around without any moral definition, not everything is permissible, but the world is a place where our instincts for goodness and our horror at evil actually make sense. We live in a moral world. They were also realistic about human selfishness and capacity for evil. Talking about how our moral behaviour is about what is within us, rather than just what we look like outside, Jesus said, 'For from the heart come evil thoughts, murder, adultery, all sexual immorality, theft, lying, and slander.' Jesus loves sinners, but he never shies away from naming reality.

The main reason, though, that Jesus and early Christian writers weren't surprised or shaken by evil had little to do with human beings. It was because they had what you could call a 'warfare worldview.' Evil, suffering and pain is partially the result of a largely unseen, but nevertheless real, battle. 'Deliver us from evil,' Jesus taught us to pray. 'The thief comes to steal, kill and destroy...I have come that you might have life.' Jesus understood that just as human beings have freedom to screw things up, so to do heavenly beings – we wrestle not against flesh and blood, but against principalities and powers that wage war against God. This might be hard to understand because we perceive it by faith, but we will simply not deal with evil unless we are able to stand against the world – by which I mean the world that tries to live as if God is not there, not to be obeyed, and floats around in its own soup of whatever morality suits it – the flesh and the devil. Why didn't Jesus blame God for the suffering of the world, and His own suffering? Why was he un-shocked by what was happening to Him, and what was going to happen to Jerusalem? Why could He trust the goodness of God in the face of banal evil? Because He knew He was fighting a battle.

Now these philosophical questions are all very well. I hope they might help convince you of the inadequacy of saying there is no god, therefore no meaning, purpose, meaning, good or evil, and the rationality of trusting in God. Joad, who I mentioned earlier, wrote a famous book in which he came round to the rationality of trusting in Christ. However, Luke does not tell us about Jesus going to the cross purely to teach us interesting stuff about the philosophy of evil.

I read this in a book about this passage. 'Jesus said, 'Do not weep for me' because Jesus was not overtaken by a fate for which He was unprepared.'

Jesus could face the cross because He was *not overtaken by a fate for which He was unprepared.*

Jesus could face this with full obedience to His father because He was not overtaken by a fate for which He was unprepared.

Jesus could deal with the horror because He was not overtaken by a fate for which He was unprepared.

One day, the reality is that something may come that shakes your life to its foundations. You may be minding your own business and suddenly you may find you are dragged into the centre of suffering and evil, forced to carry your cross, or someone else's. It might be a sorrow in your heart at the pain of the world. It might be a personal challenge or tragedy. Sooner or later we will all have to walk the same path as Jesus. In a world full of the fallout of cosmic warfare, and where sin regularly rears its ugly head, you and I must not be overtaken by a fate for which we are unprepared. When the unexpected challenge comes, like Jesus, we will only be able to say, 'Don't weep for me,' if we truly understand that while there really is evil, it is not just hopelessly 'the way things are', but it is part of living in a fallen world, where a battle is raging.

And the truly, truly great news is this. That because of the cross, evil has been trampled upon by self-sacrificial, beautiful, eternal love. Jesus defeated the powers of darkness. Jesus trusted in the victory and goodness of His father. And, because of Him, there is nothing in all creation that can separate you from God's love – nor powers, nor principalities, nor past, nor present, nor future.

The Narrative of The Cross

Torn Curtain and Centurion's Recognition

Mark 1:9-11, Mark 15:37-39
Ruth Cundy. 17th June 2018

How do you react when you start thinking about Jesus dying on the cross? Is it so familiar that really you hardly react at all? Or is there a jolt of horror every time you imagine it? Or maybe a burst of gratitude...? In the 1980's there was a film called 'Jesus' being shown all over the world. The crucifixion scene was pretty realistic, and I'm pathetically squeamish about these things. So I was horrified when I discovered that our daughter's primary school was going to show it to all the children – Sarah was 5 at the time. I talked to the head but she insisted that all the children would be expected to watch, but the teachers would try to be aware of any problems. When Sarah came home I asked her about the film. 'The teacher explained before we watched that it was only actors doing it so they weren't really hurt, they were only pretending...' I felt a moment of relief – she hadn't been too upset then. But then she paused, and added, 'But they really hurt Jesus, didn't they?' A moment of truth for a 5 year old.

Films of course exploit the blood and pain, hoping to shock us, playing on our fascination with evil and other people's pain, but have you noticed that, the gospel writers don't wallow in the details of Christ's physical suffering? Of course in no way do they diminish the horror of Jesus' physical suffering, but they do look beyond it... out of all the crucifixions at that time, what did it this one mean?

For the gospel writers, the death of Jesus was not the tragic, dramatic ending of a scene in a film – it was a moment of truth, of revelation, it marked a turning point, a new beginning... and that is really the theme of the readings and of this sermon.

Remember Mark is writing his gospel after the resurrection, after Pentecost, when he can look back and think about the deeper significance of what he saw that first Good Friday... he remembers an eerie darkness enveloping them in the middle of the day... Matthew describes an earthquake... later they would hear strange tales about the Temple curtain being torn... What was that all about?

All our sermons this year take the Cross as their starting point, and today we're looking at the significance of two important things that happened at the moment of Jesus' death – we heard them in the 2nd reading - the curtain torn in two, and the centurion's recognition of Jesus. Mark doesn't waste words – 3 short simple sentences to describe the most momentous event ever... 3 short sentences which in effect sum up the whole gospel... the turning point of history, a whole new beginning... Jesus dies, but with a cry of triumph – it is finished, completed – a new beginning can happen. The curtain is torn open to reveal God himself – we can now approach him through Jesus – a new beginning in the relationship. A representative of the world outside Judaism has a moment of revelation as he recognises Jesus as God's Son – a new beginning for all nations and cultures.

That's the gospel in a nutshell, isn't it? Christ died – our relationship with God is restored – good news for the whole world! The curtain in the Temple was hugely significant. Its origins went way back into history when the Israelites were nomads, with no settled land of their own. As they lived in tents, they made a special tent, the Tabernacle, which symbolised the presence of God travelling with them. In the centre of this tent was the Holy of Holies – a section curtained off from view. It reminded the people that Yahweh, the Lord their God was all-powerful, all-loving, all-knowing, and above all other gods worshipped by surrounding tribes. This God had a special covenant relationship with his people - and he was to be taken seriously. His 'otherness' and holiness meant no-one could approach him except the priests... hence the curtain closing off the Holy space.

Later on, the Temples built in Jerusalem, kept the same pattern... and there was still a huge heavy curtain symbolically keeping the people away from personal contact with a holy God. So the priests and Temple hierarchy had immense power over the religious life of the people, in effect granting access to God, ... and here was Jesus of Nazareth, a carpenter's son, calling God his Father, as if he had some kind of intimate relationship with him....... even worse he sometimes identified himself as the Temple itself... 'Destroy this Temple and I will raise it again in 3 days'... It was sufficiently blasphemous for the Jewish high court to ask for the death penalty...

But ironically that same death penalty they were so keen on actually meant the end of the Temple as the only way to know God... Now the way to the Father was through the Son, not through the Temple rituals... The cross became the means of reconciliation... and the relationship Jesus had with his Father could be opened up to all those who believed in him... So the tearing open of the curtain was a dramatic turning point, it marked a new beginning, a new relationship, a place where heaven and earth meet... That was extraordinary for God's people to take on board. But of course it wasn't just for them – the way was open for all who believed, Jew or Gentile, and that is why the centurion is so significant in Mark's account.

We saw earlier in the year how the gospel writers recorded Jesus' words from the cross to show us this was no ordinary crucifixion – who else in that situation of excruciating pain would utter words of compassion and forgiveness, words of triumph in the face of death? What thoughts must have been going through the mind of the centurion in all those hours of watching... Of waiting for a man to die, so the job could be over and they could all go back to barracks and have a drink... Forget about the horrors of the day job. But the centurion couldn't forget that easily... This man Jesus was different, and at that moment of death, the Roman soldier suddenly had a glimpse... an inkling... a strange insight... his own moment of truth... this man was the Son of God! Or a possible translation could be couched more in terms of his own religious background – this man was (a) son of (a) god. We don't know exactly – but for Mark himself the message is clear – for Jew and Gentile this is the Messiah, and this is a turning point in history... not just the end of a life, but a new beginning for the whole world.

Mark is choosing his words carefully here... He assumes we've read the rest of his gospel, and he wants us to make a connection – to think back to another moment of truth which marked the very beginning of Jesus' ministry in chapter 1. Where have you heard the same words before? Heaven being torn open, a voice announcing that this is God's Son. The same kind of drama but in a different context... There's a clear thread running from Jesus' baptism to his death, linking the beginning and the end of his ministry, the two most important events of his life, both marked by moments of revelation for those who can see.

At his baptism, Heaven is torn open... and God reveals himself in this image of the Spirit coming down in the form of a dove... At his death, the curtain of the Temple is torn in two... God reveals his presence unencumbered by ritual and allows us to approach him freely through Jesus...

At his baptism Jesus is affirmed as God's Son by God himself... 'You are my Son, whom I love.' At his death a Roman soldier recognises the truth... 'Surely this man was the Son of God.'

I think the challenge of Mark to us, in these two short passages, is to look for those moments of revelation, those turning points, in our own lives. Moments where in some way we encounter God... heaven is 'torn open' and God seems very real, the curtain between the sacred and the secular is torn apart... and we begin a new chapter in our relationship with him. It could be a special occasion like a baptism, or a special place where we feel God's presence; it could be listening to a sermon or studying the Bible and the Holy Spirit reveals a new truth to us; it could be when we are praying, or someone is praying for us; it could be in ordinary, everyday life... it's probably different for each of us... the important thing is that we recognise Him in those moments.

Mark's aim as he writes his gospel is that all this will be true for us, his readers, that we will encounter God through Jesus. Mark is a passionate evangelist, not an academic historian. The gospels are not history books, they're not even biographies – they are unashamedly biased accounts of a unique person, Jesus of Nazareth, Son of God, God incarnate – the Jewish Messiah, the Saviour of the world. The gospel writers want you to believe this too, they want you/me to have that moment of revelation like the centurion, when we know for certain who Jesus is, whether we fully understand the implications or not. They want us to hear God saying to us too: 'You are my son, you are my daughter whom I love.'

Where are you in this story? Where am I? Can we pray for a turning point, a new beginning in our relationship with our loving Father?

The Diamond of the Cross

Total Forgiveness
Amazing Grace
Draw Near to God
Redeemed: No more Curse of the Law
Ransomed.
The Paradox of the Cross
Once, For All
No more Sacrifice Needed
The Powers Disarmed
Slavery Ended
True Power
God has No Split Personality
It's Personal

The Diamond of the Cross

Total Forgiveness

1 John 1:1-10.
Guy Donegan-Cross. 24th June 2018

The Cross is the abyss of wonders, the centre of desires, the school of virtues, the house of wisdom, the throne of love, the theatre of joys, and the place of sorrows; It is the root of happiness, and the gate of Heaven.

We are now beginning a journey when we look at what God does through the cross through different angles – angles that are explored through letters in the New Testament.

Sometimes we try and simplify the cross, and boil it down to one simple formula. But the truth is that it is much richer than that – there are many ways to receive what Jesus achieved through the cross, and those different ways of seeing may be more important at different seasons of your life.

What applies to everyone, at all times, though, is that the cross means forgiveness. A remedy for sin. And that's where we start today.

As well as a gospel, John wrote letters. And in these letters John is trying to get across this: God really, really wants a relationship with you. He is loving, just, faithful, forgiving, constant...and He really, strongly, profoundly wants a relationship with you.

Right at the beginning of the letter he says, 'I'm not making this up! You can trust this...' 'That which was from the beginning, which we have heard, which we have seen with our eyes, which we have looked at and our hands have touched...' People are always asking, 'Where's the evidence that God loves us? That He died for us? That he really, really wants a relationship with us? John says, 'We saw him, and touched, him...'

Do you notice a word that keeps coming up again and again?

Proclaim. In other words declare something forcefully.

It's like, we are going to have a hard time receiving this so John is saying, through a megaphone, 'This is the Word of Life!' God really, really wants fellowship with you!'

As we have said before, Christians are realists. We can't make God in our own image. We can't have a relationship with God on our own terms. God has shown us what needs dealing with if we are to have a relationship with Him. He has shown us what the cross means...and that is sin. The s_ word.. We need to grapple with it, we need to understand it. Because we will not experience His grace, fellowship or love if we don't. We will walk in darkness.

If we say we have no sin...so, what is it? Rob Bell, in his book 'What is the Bible?' unpacks a great definition.

Sin is culpable disturbance of shalom.

Let's look at those words.

Shalom. Shalom is the Hebrew word for peace, wholeness, health, and blessing. Shalom is the harmony God intends for the world. Shalom is how God wants things to be. Shalom is peace with yourself, with your neighbour, with the earth, with God.

Disturbance. Things aren't how they're supposed to be, are they? From environmental degradation to domestic violence to Wall Street corruption to the petty little ways we disrespect each other, this world isn't everything it could be.

Culpable. Guilt, responsibility, ownership—culpable is any way you have contributed to the disturbance of shalom we see all around us.

Sin is anything we do to disrupt the peace and harmony God desires for the world.

Here's the problem with how many understand the word: When sin is understood primarily in terms of breaking or violating or disobeying, there's no larger context to place it in. There's whatever you did or didn't do, and then there's God's anger or wrath or displeasure with you.

But when you place it in the larger context of the good, the peace, the shalom that we all want for the world, then it starts to make way more sense. Of course I'm guilty of disturbing shalom. Is there any sane person who wouldn't own up to that?

If that is what sin means, John is saying there are two mistakes we can make.

We can make sin out to be not that important. 6 If we claim to have fellowship with him and yet walk in the darkness, we lie and do not live out the truth. In other words, if you try to love God, but don't acknowledge your need for forgiveness, you don't get it. We are either not seeing God for who He is, or we are not seeing ourselves for who we are.

The other mistake John says we can make is even more foolish, though. Twice he says, 'If we claim to be without sin, we deceive ourselves and the truth is not in us. ...If we claim we have not sinned, we make him out to be a liar and his word is not in us.'

Some people don't need convincing of this. They are acutely aware that they have screwed up. They know they have disturbed the shalom of God's world, and are culpable for it.

They are crying out for liberation, for shame and guilt to be taken away. Look at the woman who washed Jesus' feet with her tears.

But other people are more like this...they don't walk around with a sense of guilt or shame about anything really. They think they are pretty good people, most of the time. They maybe don't think it is unimportant, and maybe they know they have sinned in a theoretical sense, but they are a bit wary of the term. They are wary too of making people hate themselves, creating false guilt.

It seems to me there are two things to watch out for. One is an attitude that says, 'I am terrible. I am a miserable sinner. I am dark. I am unredeemable...Everything about me is wicked.' People who get depressed can get into that place. The other mistake is to say, 'I am me! That's all that matters. There is nothing about me that needs judging, putting right, or condemning. It doesn't really matter what I do, as long as I am happy.' Don't you just see that everywhere?

The answer is not to deny sin, or to wallow in guilt, but to live in the middle. Of course you must love yourself. But if it's at the expense of being realistic it's just narcissism. And of course you must not hate yourself. But you need a real sense of responsibility for your choices and actions before God. Russian author Solzhenitsyn said, 'The line separating good and evil passes not through states, nor between classes, nor between political parties either -- but right through every human heart -- and through all human hearts.'

There is a story in Luke when the disciples have been fishing all night without catching anything. Jesus tells them to push out into deep water, and their nets are suddenly full. Peter sees the beauty and power of Jesus and throws himself in front of him saying, 'Master leave, I am a sinner and can't handle this holiness. Leave me to myself.' When you see God's power, character and authority the charade is over. You know that if you say you are without sin, you are deceiving yourself. It's in the light of seeing who God truly is that all our narcissism can fall away.

It's a good, necessary thing to have a sense of your sin. An evangelist was one sitting at table with someone who said, 'Do you know I don't think I ever have a sinful word, deed or thought.' The evangelist picked up his glass and threw his water all over the man. 'What the hell did you do that for?' the man spluttered furiously. 'Ah, I thought the old devil might still be lurking in there,' he said.

A final thought on sin from Rob Bell, A question: What is rape?

If I told you that rape is something that is not nice, how would you respond? Or if I told you that it's really helpful when people rape less, what would you say? Or if I told you that rape just isn't the best thing that a person can do ...
Please tell me you're crawling out of your skin right about now. Why? Because I didn't use words that are strong enough and adequate enough to describe just how evil and horrific rape is.

Some words are strong for a reason. We need them to describe realities that demand that kind of strong language. Sin is one of those words. Let's keep it.

God desperately wants a loving permanent relationship with you. But your sin is a defining reality.

The cross is the remedy. The blood of Jesus. Why blood? Not because of its association with pain. But because blood carries life. In shedding it, Jesus gives away His life to us. Nothing can so dramatically convey to us the seriousness of the problem, but the completeness of the remedy.

The world might acknowledge the problem. But the solution is, 'Try harder!' To my mind that creates neurotic people. The blood of Jesus forgives. Every time. The world might say, 'Deny your guilt. Live in freedom. Love you as you.' But that is both unrealistic and narcissistic. The blood of Jesus forgives every time.

But look at what else the blood of Jesus does. John says it twice. ... the blood of Jesus, his Son, purifies us from all sin. 8 If we claim to be without sin, we deceive ourselves and the truth is not in us. 9 If we confess our sins, he is faithful and just and will forgive us our sins and purify us from all unrighteousness.

The blood of Jesus forgives us. But also purifies us. In other words, restores us to a place where it is as if what we have done never actually happened in the first place.

He dissolves it away. In his blood you are no longer the failure, the adulterer, the liar, the gossip, the hypocrite, the addict, the hate-driven, the self-absorbed. When the blood of Jesus was shed for you, all that was dissolved away. You are released from shame, from guilt. You wear white robes. You have a ring put on your finger. A banquet spread out for you. It is as if it never happened. The blood of Jesus purifies. Again and again. It's an ongoing verb tense!

Listen: I proclaim to you:

God is Light. There is no part of him that is darkness. There is nothing you have done, will do, or can do, that cannot be purified. He really, really wants to love you forever. His character is totally light. Totally love. There is no hidden part of him. It's proved by blood. He just gives life. You don't need to bargain with him. Play games with his love to test him out. I declare to you forcefully that God wants utter fellowship with you. And that Jesus' blood is all you need.

People who say, 'Great, God purifies me...now I can go out and sin again...it doesn't matter how I live...'... they just haven't seen how beautiful it is yet. They haven't received it. Because if they had, why would they *want* to do anything except love this God, who is light, who sheds His blood?

In the Bible, there's only one kind of sin—the kind that God has forgiven in Christ. May you walk in the light, knowing yourself made pure by the blood of Christ.

The Diamond of the Cross

Amazing Grace

Ephesians 2:1-10
Guy Donegan-Cross. 1st July 2018

There is a before and after in the story of the world, and there can be a before and after in the story of your life. And that before and after is around the death and resurrection of Christ.

Before that event, the world was one way. After it, nothing is the same.

Where was the world before the cross and resurrection? A place of spiritual death. And I say that because what is there about this small planet that can give spiritual life in the face of death? Before the cross what is there that could have given any hope that life is more than just a brief moment, surrounded by darkness? And before the cross what is there that could deal with the sins, greed, and selfishness which can so easily distort? And before the cross what was there that could deal with the reality of spiritual evil – what the Bible calls the ruler of the air?

Paul says that before the cross we, and you, only followed the ways of the world. Well, what else is there to follow? He says we were dead in our transgressions – if you like, our mistakes – and our sins – the things we do to muck things up, to disturb the beauty of God's wholeness. Dead because there was nothing in ourselves that can stop the rot. And, in this context, when we had no hope for the future, and no way of seeing a way out, all we can do is go where our appetites take us. Or rather, where our distorted appetites take us.

Every worldview tries to answer three questions: Where am I? What's the problem? And what's the solution? In Paul's letter we are not on a random speck of dust, but on a beautiful creation. Yet, the problem is, that before the cross we lived as if this is all there is, pushing God off the throne, grasping onto life as if we are at the centre of it, spiritually dead because we have no way of bringing ourselves to life, and at the mercy of any spiritual influence that might want to have its way with us.

So, what is the solution? Because if things are that serious, there had better be a solution that can deal with it decisively. You may not agree, or identify with any of what I've just said. You may look at the world and think, 'This is just how it's meant to be.' You may look at yourself, and think, 'I'm fine as I am.' All I can tell you is that for myself there was a day when I really, really knew I needed a Saviour. That there was potential in me – to love, to live, to be free – that needed to be set free from my propensity to hurt other people, and to tell God where to go. The words that we are 'children of wrath' are strong, aren't they? But if wrath is more like the grief of pure love in the face of the pain of the world, then, yes, I can understand that naturally I seem to have a life and a heart that would need some sorting out when standing in the presence of that love. I knew that there had to be more to life, and that something needed to happen to bring me to life. If you are not there, the cross makes little sense.

We were spiritually dead. I was spiritually dead. What's the solution? It comes, Paul says, from a God who is of great love, rich in mercy, kind, graceful. God's grace, Paul, says, opened up a whole new way to understand life. Because when Jesus died on the cross, all that stuff died with Him. That was the moment when everything changed. And to those who are willing to receive it by trusting in God – God never forces His gift on us - God joins our dead lives to Jesus, so that we share in his resurrected life...And God raised us up with Christ...we are no longer living under the shadow of shame or guilt, or of death, because what is true of Jesus is now true of us...

And when you receive this offer where does this now place your life? Well, if our lives are joined to Jesus' we are now seated with Him in the heavenly realms...it doesn't mean we sit on clouds, it means the remit of our lives is not to be a brief candle which is snuffed out, but a human being, with divine dignity, God's handiwork, God's partner, with good works, and joy, and purpose which is eternal.

One poet puts it like this:

Because he is risen
My future is an epic novel
Where once it was a mere short story
My contract on life is renewed
in perpetuity
My options are open-ended
My travel plans are cosmic
Because he is risen

Because he is risen
Healing is on order and assured
And every disability will bow
Before the endless dance of his ability
And my grave too will open
When my life is restored
For this frail and fragile body
Will not be the final word
on my condition
Because he is risen

There are so many shifts in your life that are made possible...because of this one event.

From sin to good works

From this present world to the heavenly realms

From bondage to victory with Christ

From selfish autonomy to union with Christ

From domination by the devil to a life controlled from start to finish by God

From what we are by nature to what we become by grace

From liability to God's wrath to the experience of his mercy

We are a new humanity that shares Christ's destiny and triumph and already experiences the life of heaven – God's work, created anew to live the life of goodness he has designed for it.

The cross takes us from the very lowest to the very highest!

But, brothers and sisters, God doesn't want us to know this in our heads, but to experience it in our lives. Personally. Deeply. Transformationally.

But in doing this we come up against our biggest problem – a bigger problem than anything outlined thus far. Our biggest problem is this:
Ephesians 2:5: it is by grace you have been saved.
Ephesians2:7: in order that in the coming ages he might show the incomparable riches of his grace.
Ephesians2:8: For it is by grace you have been saved, through faith—and this is not from yourselves, it is the gift of God-not by works, so that no one can boast.

God is a God of grace. Unconditional grace. We don't earn it. We don't deserve it. We don't gain it by our behaviour. This is a big problem!

We like reward. We like fairness. In fact, we get annoyed if people are rewarded for things they don't deserve. From an early age we are taught, 'You should get what you deserve.' And, 'It's not fair!' is one of our first childhood phrases. Religion operates around the rule of quid pro quo. You do this, and I'll do that.

We prefer a *contract* to a free gift, because we don't like being charity. We like giving charity, but we generally feel uneasy about receiving it.

For the early part of my Christian life, although I believed Jesus' death was for me, I resonated with this paragraph, 'I was in that same phase of trying to discipline myself to 'behave' as if I loved light and not 'behave' as if I loved darkness. I used to get really ticked about preachers who talked too much about grace, because they tempted me to not be disciplined. I figured what people needed was a kick in the butt, and if I failed at godliness it was because those around me weren't trying hard enough. I believed if word got out about grace, the whole church was going to turn into a brothel. I was a real jerk, I think.'

I simply could not believe in my soul that it wasn't about me. I thought I had to do something. And this had two bad effects: it made me feel constantly guilty and always not good enough. I always wanted to be a good Christian, but couldn't, and therefore couldn't really live in the freedom Jesus bought.

The other problem, the main one, was that it turned my relationship with God not into one of love, but of contract. Imagine if my marriage, for example, functioned like this.

So Ruth, I just thought I'd see if I'm deserving of your love today...Could we just compare points?

Sure. So far, I am pretty much the perfect wife. I made supper last night – spinach cannelloni – very time consuming – worth five points on the marriage index; washed up because you were busy doing good – that's another five – and I laughed at three of your jokes – that's got to be another ten points. I think I've done pretty well in fulfilling my side of the marriage with 20 points. So what have you got?

Um...OK. So I walked Bess twice today...

That's one point each. You enjoy doing that.

OK.

I noticed your new blouse and commented appreciatively?

One.

I made a packed lunch for Anna.

Well, that's only three points...

Oh, come on. It says in clause 4 that if I do something I hate that doubles points!

All right...well, you are up to nine. I had twenty.

I'm getting there...What a great marriage we have, don't we?

We would never see a marriage that functions like this as being natural or life-giving. This constant anxiety to deserve the other person's love...

So why do we find it so hard to experience God's unconditional, merciful, kind offer of new life through the cross of Christ? A cross that alone can take us from the lowest spiritual death to the highest sense of human purpose and destiny?

When we listen to the voice in our ear that tells us we don't deserve this, that we are losers, that we are failures whom God only tolerates, we are believing the opposite of the cross. When we see that the cross is God's free gift, we will experience and enjoy the love he offers. We will only love God, because He first loves us, and obey God because we love Him.

Here, today, is the event, the moment around which everything hangs. And here today, is the love poured out that is the only motive for us wanting to obey Him in return.

The Diamond of the Cross

Draw Near to God

Ephesians 2:11-22
Guy Donegan-Cross. 8th July 2018

In Ephesians Paul is writing to a group of Christians and in the first half of the letter saying, 'Because of the cross, this is who you are now. You were that. And now you are this.' In the second half of the letter he tells them how they live that out. But here we are in the thick of the first half, finding out who we are through Jesus. Last week we saw how through His amazing grace, and through his grace alone, we have been raised to life with Christ. We were dead, but now, because we are joined to Him, in His death and resurrection, we have a new identity, seated with Christ. Once your life was dead: a mere short story. But through Jesus we can have a future which is an epic novel!

Jesus changed everything for each of us with God. Forever. But, just as profoundly, the cross means we never look at one another in the same way ever again.

Paul says at one time there were different sets of people, alienated from each other. There were the Jews, who were called to be a blessing to the nations, who had a covenant relationship with God. They had to be holy, to be set apart for God's purposes. God had given them a special calling, which Gentiles didn't share, but the whole idea was that they would show His love through being a light to the world. They were very good at making themselves a distinct people, they had their own services, rituals and customs (including circumcision), but the bitter irony was that this became the opposite of what was intended. They made God into their property, and excluded others. It got so pronounced that there was a wall around their temple in Jerusalem which had notices on it that read, 'Trespassers will be executed.' And if a Jewish son married a Gentile daughter, the Jewish family would have a funeral for their son. That's who they were.

So when Paul says there was a dividing wall of hostility, it wasn't just a metaphor. And this sorry situation is like history written in miniature. It's a description of the way human beings retreat into nationalism and self-defensiveness. Of course, this is a huge issue right now. Apart from climate change, the biggest issue in terms of our relationship to the world is how we see the role of national identity today. Migration, Brexit, detentions, multicultural questions, what you can't and can wear, border walls...they all have their roots in the same very human questions Paul is asking. We live in a world where the cocktail of a merging of identities, and a scarcity of resources is asking us to respond very quickly to the question of who is in and who is out, and how should the outsider and the different.

This may not be theoretical for you. You may either feel threatened by these questions, but genuinely want to know what a Jesus shaped response is. Or you might feel excluded – from society, from God or from the church.

Paul is really clear what the cross has done. And it's both good news personally, and a shining light to the world right now. The old city of Antioch used to be literally divided by walls, with 18 ethnic quarters there. The high walls between every ethnic area would protect the groups from each other. Then the gospel came to Antioch through persecution. Here, for the first time they were called Christians – for the first time in history. Why? Because people were crossing the walls to worship together. Their identity was no longer about ethnic division, but about Christ. They were Christ-ians above all!

Peace between people. Three times Paul says the cross means peace. Most people in the world want peace, and the cross gives a peace which is deeper than that formed by self-interest, and eternal.

How does the cross make peace? Firstly, because at the cross there is no longer any 'in crowd'. I've always wanted to be in the in crowd. I think we are wired for it. And of course, being in the in crowd automatically means you define yourself as opposite to the out crowd. In crowds can particularly come together round a particular person. If you can't be the centre of the in crowd the next best thing is to have access to them. This is me meeting Princess Anne. I was invited to her house. How did I get there? Well, obviously she rang me up one day...No, the truth is that I knew someone – in this case my headteacher – who invited me in to her presence. I asked her about horses. Anyway, the point is there were only a few of us who got in. And that made me feel special, different from others.

For those of you seething with jealousy, and feeling left out, or who are already cueing up your story of how you met someone special (so you are even more in than me!) I've got good news. You're already in the in crowd. In fact, we all are. There is no one who is excluded. Through Jesus we've got access not to Princess Anne, but to God the Father. We are all equally, wonderfully, brought into his presence not by a headteacher by the son of God. Because we can be assured that we can not just know about the father, but know him personally and intimately, we can also be sure that we are no more or less than anybody else in the world. If you are an Iranian Christian, or a Pakistani Christian, or a British Christian, Catholic, a Methodist or whatever, we are all given peace with God through access to the father.

Look at these footballers praying in the world cup. Is the thing that binds them together the fact that they come from the same country or play on the same team? Partially. But the main thing that binds them is that at the touch line they all have access to the Father.

Jesus gives us this through the cross and makes us equal. But he also makes us equal by taking something away from us. Jesus is our peace who has made one new humanity in himself, in one body, putting to death any hostility. And how has he done this? By taking away everything we glory in, everything we big ourselves up in, everything we place our identity in, and making it irrelevant compared to the fact that we are the ones he has died for. The only thing that matters from now on is who we are at the cross, through the cross, in the cross. This is the great leveller. All the things that we glory in - success, our wealth, our privilege - all the things in other words that exclude us from one another - are rendered redundant by the beauty of the cross.

Don't get me wrong. It's great to be English. Well three quarters English actually. God created a world of variety. Cultural differences, like Elgar, Betty's tea, cricket and Love Island are all marvellous expressions of the variety of God's creation. Different languages, customs, music, art, social rituals can be a great blessing. At the end of the Bible we don't see people losing their cultural identity, or language, but all praising God together with all those differences.

The Greek word for church is ekklesia, called out, but you're not called out of involvement with the world. You're called out of the identity. That's the reason why you can say you're a Christian first and you're English, or Indian, or Chinese second. It's also a reason why Christians are the least culturally bound of any religion. Most religions tend to be strongly rooted within a particular language, or people, or tribe. They are very strongly associated with ethnicity. Christians aren't. The good news of the cross has taken root in every culture. Because it's not about culture or ethnicity. Those walls have been taken down.

So here are a few questions to finish with. Do you know you are no longer a foreigner or a stranger, but have been brought near, given access to the Father like everyone else? Or do you think of yourself as outside? Jesus died to bring you in. And not just to know it in your head, but to breathe in the peace of knowing God. There is knowing in your head. But then there is living. Ruth had a prang in the car last week. And I just want to make it clear, it wasn't her fault! Before the prang she knew the highway code, the speed limit, safe distance – as head knowledge. Now, that information is affecting her driving completely. May your knowledge of the Father bring a *transforming* peace.

Do you know, too, that you are a member of God's household? His family? A family built on Jesus, where there is no hierarchy. I am passionate about the Harrogate Hub, about being one family on mission together. About making visible the reality of what Jesus has done on the cross by tearing down the walls between churches. If the only thing we do is demonstrate that unity, it is a sign of the cross.

When we are unified like this Paul says we become a holy temple in the Lord, built together to become a dwelling in which God lives by his Spirit. But this is a temple without walls. A temple that has the prophetic task of resisting and tearing down walls of hostility that the world puts up.

We should rejoice in our culture, but we should hold onto national identity very, very lightly. If you think about it, what does national identity often coalesce around? If you are English it's 'Rule Britannia,' Trafalgar, the Spirit of Dunkirk, and 'Never Surrender.' Nationalist ways of defining yourself are flimsy because they can so easily be formed around memories of defeating your enemies. And name me one state anywhere in the world that contains only one people of one nation anyway?

We are instead a holy nation, whose fortress is a faithful heart, whose pride is suffering; and as the truth of the cross is revealed, soul by soul and silently her shining bounds increase, a new humanity is formed, and her ways are ways of gentleness, and all her paths are peace. We have a calling to resist at every point the fear and self-defensiveness of nationalist thinking. Let's be part of God's future, where the flag flying over us is only His love, His love binding us together through the cross.

The Diamond of the Cross

Redeemed: No more Curse of the Law

Galatians 3:10-14
Guy Donegan-Cross. 15th July 2018

The preacher John Stott told a story about an Eastern European couple who moved to Western Europe and received their first wedding invitation. It read, 'You are cordially invited to the wedding of so and so, at such and such a time. RSVP.' The couple fretted for a long time and the husband asked his wife, 'Vife, vat is dis RSVP?' 'I don't know husbvand.' After a long time of pondering and code-breaking, the husband threw his hands up in the air and proclaimed his epiphany. 'I know vat it means! REMEMBER SOME VEDDING PRESENTS.'

The couple had confused the invitation with a demand.

The cross is an invitation to freedom, peace and joy. It's an invitation as Paul says to receive the blessing given to Abraham. What did Abraham receive? A covenant relationship with God – His promise forever.

But whereas the cross is an invitation to life, human beings can receive it, and create religions, which are all about command, keeping regulations, living in fear of not being up to the mark.

This is the curse of living under the law. Anyone who confuses the invitation of God with the demand of God will end up being in a Catch 22. They will be constantly trying to do their best, never being able to quite be up to the mark. Because everyone who does not continually keep the law knows that it is a hard taskmaster. It's a kind of spiritual slavery. And the really sad thing is that the more you try and please God through your own efforts, the more you live into the idea that God is a slave-driver, rather than the Father of love.

This performance anxiety faith is still endemic, even amongst Christians. It stems from the way that primitive religions all thought worship was about making sure the harvests came. If we worshipped and sacrificed enough then maybe we could stop the gods being angry, and they would provide for us. But you never quite knew if you had done enough. Of course, the more extreme versions involved human sacrifice, something that God showed Abraham in a most dramatic way that He did not want.

But this tendency to keep going back to a slave-mentality is a constant threat. And it's the opposite of what Jesus came to do through the cross. These Christians in Galatia still have a slave-mentality, still trying to put conditions on themselves and each other by insisting that some people can only be proper Christians if they obey this or that regulation. He lets his frustration boil over. 'You crazy Galatians! Did someone put a hex on you? Have you taken leave of your senses? Something crazy has happened, for it's obvious that you no longer have the crucified Jesus in clear focus in your lives. His sacrifice on the cross was certainly set before you clearly enough. Let me put this question to you: How did your new life begin? Was it by working your heads off to please God? Or was it by responding to God's Message to you? Are you going to continue this craziness? For only crazy people would think they could complete by their own efforts what was begun by God.'

Can I ask you: are you a crazy Christian? Are you working your head off to please God? Or can you put the crucified Jesus in clear focus in front of you so you can be free? To be a Christian is an invitation never to be a slave again.

Christ, it says, redeemed us, redeemed you. He is your precious redeemer. Imagine you are standing on block in a slave market, chained. Maybe you have put yourself there, unable to pay your debts. The one who redeems you is the one who pays for your freedom, and lets you go. A free person. No longer a slave. It's a free gift. And while He is your master, even though He frees you, He does not force you to serve Him – only if you want to. Because there is nothing left to pay.

Redemption is like the famous painter who returned to his home town one day and passing an antique shop saw one of his own paintings in the window. It was not what it was – the paint was peeling and the frame broken. He went into the shop and bought it back. Taking it home he restored and reframed it, so that the effects of years of neglect were no longer there...While most religion is about what we do, act, perform, Christianity is only about what God has done through the cross to buy us out of slavery.

There is however, always a cost. Redemption doesn't just mean rescuing. It means rescuing at a price. Christ redeemed us from the curse of the law by becoming a curse for us. It is like he freed us from the slave market not with a bag of gold, but by becoming a slave, taking on the chains, and becoming nothing. Paul says in Philippians explicitly, 'he made himself nothing by taking the very nature of a slave...he humbled himself by becoming obedient to death—even death on a cross!'

The invitation is to freedom – from the curse of trying to be good, and always failing. Free from a slave-driver God. You have been redeemed! Don't turn an invitation to life into a command to slavery again. Jesus' redemption is uniquely not an invitation to do more good works as a way of justifying yourself, but only an invitation to live by trusting His love. When you fail, sin, fall, stumble, trust in His sweet redemption. You were bought at a price. To be a Christian is not to be connected to good works, or to church, or to outward ritual, or to success, but only to be connected to Christ. To trust Him. Full stop.

God wants to free people. And the more we are freed, the more our love for Him will motivate us to see others freed.

The Diamond of the Cross

Ransomed

1 Peter 1:18-21, John 3:13-17
John Duff. 22nd July 2018

Praise my Soul the King of heaven,
to his feet thy tribute bring,
ransomed, healed, restored, forgiven,
who like thee his praise would sing.

This is a familiar hymn to many of us I'm sure. We are probably Ok with healed, restored, forgiven....but ransomed?

How is the cross a ransom?

If you are confused – you are in good company, after 2000 years Christians don't agree exactly what it means.

In NT times paying a 'ransom' to return war captives was common practice.
In Mark Jesus says 'For the Son of Man did not come to be served but to serve and give his life a ransom for many.'

In his letter to Timothy Paul writes that Jesus gave his life as a ransom.
So ransom is associated with the transfer of ownership of a captive on payment of a price.

Where Christians disagree is who or what the ransom is paid to.
Some suggest due to sin the devil is our master and the ransom was paid to him.
Some suggest that death is our master.
Some suggest it is freedom from slavery to sin, where sin is our master.

Some suggest it is to God to satisfy his justice and the law is our master.
I just don't know.

What all agree on and is more relevant to us is the level of the ransom payment.

Peter tells us that silver was not enough, gold was not enough, and only the blood of Christ could buy us back. The most precious commodity in the universe – the life of Jesus paid on the cross, paid, as it were, on the nail. John tells us that God loved the world so much He gave His only Son that whoever believes in Him should not die but have eternal life. There is a business principle which states: 'something is only worth as much as someone is prepared to pay to own it.' If you have ever tried selling a house, or selling on eBay you will see how relevant that principle is.

How much are you worth to God?

You are worth the life of Jesus – the most precious commodity in the universe.

But bear in mind....

So is Donald Trump and the children he has separated from their parents.
So is Bashar al Assad and the people his armies have maimed and killed.
So is every Israeli and every Palestinian.
So is your family.
So is the person who annoys you most.
So are you.

You are worth as much as God was willing to pay as a ransom that you could be his.

Ransomed, healed, restored, forgiven
Who like thee his praise should sing?

The Diamond of the Cross

The Paradox of the Cross

Romans 5:6-10, Luke 9:21-27
Dan Watts. 9th September 2018

Who or what would you be willing to die for?

My guess is that you may well have said a child, a spouse of possibly another family member or close friend. We can imagine being willing to die for another person that we dearly love because almost certainly they will love us too. I wonder if there was anyone here prepared to die for a particular cause? Brexit, Gareth Southgate for prime minister or being an ambassador/witness for Jesus?

In today's reading we read 'very rarely will anyone die for a righteous person, though for a good person someone might possibly dare to die.' Rarely will a person give his or her life for someone they merely respect, someone who is righteous; but occasionally a person dies for the sake of someone they love, someone who is good.

The awesome quality of God's love for us is seen in that Christ died for us while we were 'still sinners.' Paul tells us that Christ died for us when we were powerless, ungodly, sinners and enemies of God. There's a progression in these terms from bad to worse. We were not just powerless; we were ungodly. And we were not just ungodly; we were sinners. And we were not only sinners; we were God's enemies.

It is almost impossible for us to think we are being loved when we are hurting. We feel broken, we feel worthless, and we feel forgotten. That is why we need to understand the argument in Verses 6 through 10. Paul says there is a place where every

Christian knows that God loves him, even though he himself is worthless, useless and forgotten. What is that place? It is the cross. In the cross of Jesus Christ you always see two things: First, you see yourself and second you see the full extend of God's love for you.

You see, as Paul puts it here, that you are helpless. If there were any other way to get to God, then there never would have been a cross. But the cross is God's testimony that there is no other way. That is why it says, 'At the right time, Christ died.' The Greek word for time in this verse is '*Kairos*', which simply means 'opportune moment, the appointed time, the right time.' At that time in history God amply demonstrated to the entire world that man could not save himself and so He sent His son Jesus to die on the cross in our place and reveal the full extent of His love. God's love for His own is unwavering because it is not based on how lovable we are, but on the constancy of His own character. God's supreme act of love came when we were at our most undesirable.

The great Hebrew prophets had spoken, and that didn't help. Greek philosophers had taught, and that didn't help. The Romans had come in with their military might, and law and order was imposed over the course of the whole known world of that day, and that didn't help. *But* at the right time, Christ died on the cross so that men could see how helpless and powerless they were to save themselves. 'The spectacle of the cross, the most public event of Jesus life, reveals the vast difference a god who proves himself through power and One who proves himself through love,' writes Philip Yancey.

As we look at the cross we see how ungodly we are. We are not like God; we don't act like God. We have the capacity to do so, but we don't. We even want to at times, but we don't. Therefore, we see in the cross how unlike God we are. We see that we are sinners. We are involved in things that are hurtful. We are destroying ourselves and others. We find ourselves lawless and selfish at times, and we know it was man's sin -- our sin, yours and mine -- that nailed Jesus to that cross. It was not His own sin, but yours and mine. There we learn that we are enemies of God, enemies sabotaging God's plan to help us, wrecking everything he tries to do to reach us. For years we fight back and resist God's efforts to love us and to draw us to himself. We are the enemies of God.

Can you believe that – when you were God's enemy – Jesus died for you? To bring you back into relationship with God the Father, the One who created you. Jesus died so that you would be forgiven for your sin. Not only are you forgiven but He also declares you innocent and absolves you from any punishment that your sin rightly deserves. On the cross Jesus bears your guilt and shame, he pays the price for your sin so that you can go free and enter into a loving relationship with your Father in heaven.

Wow. Did you get that? Jesus died for you and me when we were his enemies. When we hated him; when we didn't know our need of him; when we thought we could do life without him; when we turned our back on him and walked away. Jesus died for us when we were unlovable and incapable of loving Him back.

Yet we know, if we are Christians at all, that in that place where man's inadequacy is so fully demonstrated, we also have the clearest testimony that God loves us. 'God so loved the world that he gave his one and only Son,' (John 3:16). Jesus came to break through all our despair and weakness and shame and sorrow and sin, all man's ruin and disaster. He came to demonstrate a God who loved mankind and would not let it perish.

Now we come to the force of Paul's argument. If you clearly knew God's love when you became a Christian -- when you were enemies and helpless and powerless -- how much more can you count on the fact that God loves you now that you are his child?

Even though you are suffering, even though you don't feel loved right now, even though it seems as though God is against you, how much more you can count on the fact that God loves you.

Paul is arguing from the greater to the lesser. If God could love you when it was so evident to you that you didn't deserve it, how much more must you reckon upon his love now that you know that you are dear to him and loved by him. If God loved us so much that Christ would die for us when we were in such a state as Paul describes, then we may have full confidence in God's love for us in the present and in the future as well. Christ died for us at just the right time.

Dali painted a picture of the cross 'Christ of St. John of the Cross', which was inspired by the sixteenth century monk John of the Cross. What makes the painting remarkable is its point of view. It is a depiction of the crucifixion from above. It is, presumably, God's view of the event. The German theologian Paul Althaus said, 'Jesus died for God before he died for us'. The act of dying is also an act of obedience, love and worship. Jesus himself said unless a seed falls to the ground and dies, it couldn't bear fruit. So it is that death and life are linked in the Christian journey. We must be willing to die both metaphorically and actually in order to see the kingdom of God in our lives. If anyone would come after me, Jesus explains, they 'must deny themselves and take up their cross and follow me.'

Jesus' own teaching was filled with irony and Paradox. 'For whoever wants to save their life will loose it, but whoever loses their life for me will find it.' He can scarcely teach without it. He issues ironic statements like these often: the first are last, enemies are loved, the slave is free, the poor are rich and the rich are poor, the meek inherit the earth and persecuted are blessed, the list goes on. The Gospel itself is ironic. God dies for sinners; he is strong enough to be weak enough to die, so that we might live. The paradox of the cross is that death brings life.

As Christians we live in the tension of paradox and irony. Are we, for instance, supposed to be content or discontent as Christians? Should we laugh or lament? Are we free in Christ or slaves to God? Is our core identity sinner or saint? Has the kingdom come, or is it coming later? Am I supposed to live an abundant life or die a martyr's death? Is the gospel something that is proclaimed or demonstrated? I guess the answer is yes to all these, we live out and embody a culture of paradox in the Kingdom of God.

When Jesus promised the Church his presence (Matthew 28:20), he also left them an identity and calling to be his witnesses. The original word for witness in Greek, '*martus*' is where we get the English word martyr because the witness Jesus was describing was a matter of life and death. In our lives, there are some people and even ideas that we are so deeply committed to, towards which we feel such profound love, that we would be willing to suffer and even die for them. Jesus calls for that kind of love, not just for him, but for each other and, perhaps more to the point, for the world that rejects us. We are his witnesses precisely because we are willing to die like him in the service of lost people. Will we lay down our lives, our careers, and our future for the sake of this great love?

In The Message of the Cross, Derek Tidball writes 'before the cross countless men and women of every generation and culture have stood in adoring wonder and humble patience. The cross stands at the very heart of the Christian faith, manifesting the love of God, effecting salvation from sin, conquering the hostile forces and inviting reconciliation with God.'

What would you be willing to die for?

The Diamond of the Cross

Once, For All

Romans 5:12-21
Guy Donegan-Cross. 16th September 2018

The passage we look at today talks a lot about Adam. It says we are all 'in Adam'. Because of what Adam did we are all affected. All to blame. Before we read it, it might be worth staking out a couple of thoughts. Firstly, do you have to believe Adam was a literal human being to understand what Paul is saying? I would briefly say that a clue might be found in this passage where Paul says, 'Adam is a pattern of the one to come.' He's a type, a metaphor, a description of a spiritual reality. You don't have to believe Genesis is a science book, or that human beings all began 10,000 years ago to make sense of this, and be faithful to interpreting it.

The second thing that might be helpful to clarify is the question related to how one person's sin against God could justifiably have such a negative impact on the rest of us. None of us asked to be born, and none of us asked to be descended from Adam. So can we really believe in a version of God that says, 'Just because of Adam's original sin, it doesn't matter if you are only a day old, but hard luck mate?' Sadly, many people have imbibed this. But the picture of God in that case is more mean, more irrational and more vindictive than any of us could be. It's a huge moral problem for us. And it doesn't even square up with some of the things the Bible itself says. For example in Ezekiel we read, 'The one who sins is the one who will die. The child will not share the guilt of the parent, nor will the parent share the guilt of the child.'

So I don't think Paul is describing God as being unfair here. He is simply stating that human beings have a big problem – one that we have to own up to, one that affects everyone, and one that we need to be real about....But, he says, the solution is far, far better than anything we can dream of. Sometimes, when you go to the doctor, the diagnosis can seem scary or difficult to understand....Aha! the doctor might say, 'I see you are 'in Adam'. Oh dear!' But a good diagnosis can only help us on the road to complete healing as we shall see.

We love the fairy story myth of rags to riches. It resonates with something deep in our souls. Being brought from the very lowest to the very highest. From sweeping up in the kitchen, dressed in workaday clothes to being swept up into the beauty of the ball and glass slippers. From zero to hero. There is a deep awareness in us that we are so much more than we could be. Am I really all I could be? Why do I keep screwing up? Being unsure of where I am? Who I am? What I am doing here?

It's good to look at yourself, before looking at others, to judge yourself, before you judge others. But this 'rags' condition is, from Paul's point of view, universal. It's all part of being 'in Adam.' It's not about your lineage, it's about your condition. In non-Western cultures, people have less of a problem with the idea that who I am affects who you are and vice versa. That we are all one organism. That we are all formed by the way other people think and behave. In South Africa there is a word, 'Ubuntu: I am because you are.' This is both a beautiful thought – we are interconnected – and also an acknowledgement that there is no such thing as one person who is disconnected from everybody else, and can therefore stand back in judgement.

So while there may not be a literal Adam, there is literal death – that affects everyone. There is literal sin, and literal disobedience. In Adam the literal truth is that everything we hold dear is temporary, that we literally can only cling on to meaning for a few short years, that we literally have no eternal value, and that in Adam alone whenever we see pain, and suffering, and sorrow all we can literally do is keep calm and carry on.

I was chatting to someone last week who was worried that a relative of hers was drinking too much, and perhaps straying into alcoholism. And yet he didn't want to listen, didn't believe there was a problem, that it is all under control. We talked about the Twelve Steps of Alcoholics Anonymous. The first step is this. 'We admitted we were powerless – that our lives had become unmanageable.' And the second step is this, 'We came to believe that a Power greater than ourselves could restore us to sanity.'

As far as Paul is concerned being in Adam isn't about saying God is unfair, or begrudging, or likes to make contracts with us. It's about a long, hard sane look at us, about our literal, universal, total human condition. To say we are all 'in Adam' is a reality check. And it's a great leveller. No one is excluded from this. Before God we are all 'in Adam'. The Archbishop of Canterbury is in Adam. I am in Adam! You are in Adam! We should avoid making each other into Christian celebrities – those people on the stage, at the conference, in the pulpit are just as much 'in Adam' as you are. And on the other hand we should cut each other some slack as well. If you are fed up with, disillusioned by, disappointed with 'the church' – whether national or local, just remember we all are dealing with the same condition. Let's be gentle with each other.

Can we just note as an extra point something that might be helpful here. Sometimes people have made the argument throughout history that men should be first, tops, and in leadership because somehow the Bible portrays women, through Eve, as being the ones who introduced sin into the world. If Eve hadn't tempted Adam, the story goes, we wouldn't be in this mess. And that's one of the theological reasons why some church communities don't allow women to lead. Apart from that being a dodgy reading of Genesis, I wonder how they respond to the idea here that it is through Adam that we all sinned, because of Adam we all die. I notice Paul didn't write that we are all in Eve. Praise God that it takes both men and women to fully image God, and that we can have men and women equally in leadership.

The reality being 'in Adam' describes is terminal, catastrophic and universal. Alienated from God, from creation, from each other and destined for death. But listen...the whole point of Paul's letter is to reveal a beautiful, gleeful, joyful, death-shattering, sin cleansing, eternity-beckoning contrast! Adam is not the final word about us! Instead through his life, death and resurrection, Jesus is the first word, the final word, the ultimate word, and the best word!

The only reason for mentioning the problem, is to show how brilliantly wonderful God's gift is. It's a bit like one of those good news/bad news jokes...I have good news and bad news about the car...What's the good news? The airbags work!....but in reverse. Yes, there is bad news, but the gift of God is so much more it cannot be compared with the effect of us being 'in Adam'.

Firstly, God's gift of forgiveness is so much greater than the effect of our sin. For those of us who struggle with a sense of failure, guilt or shame, breathe in these words: If the many died by the trespass of the one man, how much more did God's grace and the gift that came by the grace of the one man, Jesus Christ, overflow to the many!...where sin increased, grace increased all the more, 21 so that, just as sin reigned in death, so also grace might reign through righteousness to bring eternal life through Jesus Christ our Lord.

In other words, you cannot out-sin God's grace. Before the words of confession are out of your mouth He has restored you. A twelve year old accidentally killed one of his family's geese by throwing a stone. Figuring his parents wouldn't notice one of twenty-four gone he buried it. His sister saw his crime and said, 'I saw what you did, and if you don't wash the dishes for me, I'll tell mum.' The boy did the dishes for days. One day, the boy said,

'You do them.' His sister said, 'I'll tell mum.' The boy replied, 'I already told her and she forgave me – I'm free again.'

Where sin increased, grace increases more. Grace reigns. God makes you righteous. Completely able to be in right relationship with Him. Forever. When you stand before God, in Christ He will not see anything about you He does not love.

This is so important, because God's big plan is not to tweak us so we are a bit better than we were, but to completely remake us. Magazines and books, and self-help culture can only offer temporary ways of papering over all it means to be 'in Adam.' Solutions don't last because they aren't about reshaping our humanity. Our old humanity was in Adam, and led to death. God's dream for His new humanity is superabundantly more marvellous. Remade people in the image of His Son. No longer defined by the brokenness of the world, but by the glory of His Kingdom. Excuse the old language but C.S. Lewis put it well when he wrote, "The Son of God became a man to enable men to become sons of God.' That is not a tweak. That is a gift of new life.

I emerge from the tomb of my slumber
Loose the attachments
That bound me for so long
No one guessed at my beauty
I leave the stifling night of my confinement
Slide into the cool baptismal waters
Suspended in the breaking of the dawn
Stroke on stroke
Stroke on stroke
I glide
Suspended in mercy
Now I emerge
Now I breathe
Now I sing
Now I live

Your redemption

If Cinderella refused to go to the ball when her dress changed, the coach pulled up and fairy godmother sang, 'Bibbedy-bobbedy-boo' we would think her mad. Why stay in that old condition? The whole point is that we are to become new. To embrace the gift of utter change that being in Christ means. There was a lawyer who decided to cancel the debts of all his clients that had owed him money for more than 6 months. He drafted a letter explaining his decision and sent 17 debt cancelling letters. One by one, the letters were returned by the Postal Service, unsigned and undelivered. Sixteen of the seventeen letters came back to him. They could not believe how deep, how profound, how universal this gift was.

Just as Adam affected everyone, so God's offer of being remade in Christ is offered to all. The reach of God's grace is universal. Every person. Every age, culture, country, creed. But this is a non-coercive offer, which has to be received. It is universally offered, but not universally accepted.

I hope the impact of these words says to each heart here, 'Why stay in Adam, when you can die to him and live in Christ forever? Hear how much the beauty of God's love through the obedience of Christ can totally remake you.' That may be your personal journey today.

But I want to end by encouraging us all as a church community to see how our vision is all about holding this hope out to others. We are ambassadors, saying to people, 'We can be much more than this. Adam does not have the last word. In Christ, how much more the grace of God can offer life, forgiveness and hope!' In many ways our whole vision of being A 'Family of Servants on Mission' is about trying to live into this identity, and hold it out to others.

As you know we are seeking to grow communities where it is not just about meeting our needs, but about growing through doing some kind of mission together. We have one community that is reaching out by having a film night, one by doing a book club, one by engaging with people through the environment, one with a specific vision for a group of streets, one regularly visiting a residential home. Other communities are seeking a way forward...we continue to work towards growing together by serving more and more together. At the same time we are considering changing what we do on a Sunday evening – with one of the primary motives being thinking about who we can reach out to more effectively in that evening slot. We don't know the final shape yet, but recognize that any change can bring discomfort.

But we are a Family, of Servants, on Mission. We serve, and we reach out. Taking risks. Stepping out of our comfort zones for the sake of others. A new humanity, formed around Jesus. Determined to grow in sharing this good news, in being ambassadors. May each of us know in the depths of who we are that God's grace overflows to us, and makes us new. And may we have a fire to call our neighbours, our friends, our town and our nation to be found, no longer in Adam, but eternally in Christ.

The Diamond of the Cross

No more Sacrifice Needed

Hebrews 10:8-14
James Handley. 30th September 2018

Hebrews is an interesting book – we don't know when it was written, or who wrote it, or indeed who it was written to! But we can be fairly sure that it was written in the 1st century, and aimed at Jewish Christians. Its major theme is that Christians, through Christ, now have direct access to God. You and I perhaps take this for granted, but for the early Jewish Christians it would have been dynamite. Many of the laws and regulations in the Old Testament were around Israel staying pure, and dealing with sin, and enabling some form of relationship between the Israelites and God.

At the start of this year we looked at the sacrificial system in Leviticus, in which the High Priest offered sacrifices on behalf of himself, his family, and the whole of Israel, to atone for sin – or you might say to make them 'at-one' with God again. Somehow the blood of the ritually slaughtered animals made the community pure, and able to co-exist with God, at least for a time. These ritual ceremonies of atonement were a foreshadowing, or a looking forward, to Jesus' ultimate sacrifice on the cross. In Hebrews we've got to the reverse angle, looking back at the sacrificial system from the perspective of the cross. As the writer identifies, the same old sacrifice, offered over and over, again and again, can never take away sins. However 'this priest' – by which the writer means Jesus – 'has offered for all time one sacrifice for sins'.

So hooray, sin has been dealt with once and for all!

... except that it kind of hasn't, has it? I don't look around the world today and see that sin has been dealt with. If I dare say it, I don't look around this congregation, and see that sin has been dealt with. And I certainly don't look at myself and say sin has been dealt with.

So what is going on?

I think what is going on is that the cross gives us an insight into the breath-taking audacity of God's love. The cross is God's *one and only* plan for dealing with Sin – one time for ever. The cross is the offer of God to everyone – no matter what they have done in the past, and what they will do in the future – that reconciliation with God is not only possible but has already happened. Heaven is wide open. No more sacrifice is needed.

I don't know about you, but to me this sounds like an incredibly risky strategy! It's a bit like me saying to my children 'I will say "yes" to *anything* you ask'. Or going up to a random stranger on the street and saying 'Here, I'm recruiting you for my embassy, you now have complete diplomatic immunity for anything you've done in the past or will do in the future'. Actually it's more than risky, it's crazy, isn't it? Giving the offer of absolute carte blanche, for all time, to everyone, no matter what! Especially if you already know they are going to fail at it, and be self-destructive, unkind, immoral, and so on. And let's be clear – this offer costs God dearly. Jesus – who is God - chose to come and to die in order to make this crazy love plan happen. God gave up his very life, to make this offer of unconditional love. This comprehensive, once for all-time, utterly complete, dealing with of sin. At infinite cost to himself, he shows infinite love. And this is the very definition of grace.

But why – why would God do something so outrageous? The 20th century theologian C.E. Rolt talked about divine omnipotence (the idea that God is all powerful). It is possible to understand omnipotence in terms of coercive power – that God has infinite brute force, i.e. 'God can do whatever God wants' – but Rolt dismisses this thinking as immoral, irrational, and anti-Christian!

Rather, Rolt sees God's power as the very opposite – Instead of force, it is the ability with withstand any opposing force with patient endurance, hoping and waiting, until this opposing force is won over by love.

> 'heavenly power cannot crush opposing forces;
> it can only suffer and be crushed by them. It
> cannot break or bend anything to its will; it can
> only be bent and broken yet remain
> unconquered'

God's master plan, His Plan A, in fact His *only* plan, is to try and win us over with His love. He has taken the initiative, in dealing with sin once and for all, as an unconditional offer of love to you and to me. No more sacrifice is needed.

Now don't get me wrong - I'm not suggesting that our sin doesn't have consequences, and indeed we know this is the case just by looking around us. We are still living in a world where Sin and Death rule. And God cares deeply about righteousness and justice – far more than we do actually. But – if we allow ourselves to be loved by God, and love him back – we can start to live *now* in the world which is *still to come*, where Love rules, and Sin and Death are no more. I'm not suggesting that we don't need to repent - to have *metanoia*, the change of heart and mind. But I am saying that Sin and Death have been beaten, once and for all, and you and I are invited to live in this new world. This now/not yet tension is perhaps what is trying to be captured in verse 14 'For by one sacrifice he has made perfect forever those who are being made holy.' We *are* made perfect forever, yet are still *being made* holy.

And as we are increasingly 'made holy' and live in this world that is yet to come, I think that the consequences of sin *are* diminished. We begin to bring this new world into existence, in a way. And the great joy is that is us the Church – the community of believers – who are the primary expression of this new world. As we are recklessly loved by God, so we begin to recklessly love others. 'Forgive us our sins, as we forgive those who sin against us'. Sin and Death say that when you hurt me, I hurt you back (or at least avoid you over coffee)... and Sin and Death multiply. Reckless love says that when you do something that hurts me, I forgive you and love you... and Sin is defeated. Sin and Death say 'I deserve to live in a nice house, with nice clothes, and nice food to eat.' Reckless love says '22,000 children will die today around the world because of poverty - how can I share what I have in abundance with those who have nothing?' Reckless love costs, and it hurts. It cost and it hurt Jesus. And it will cost and hurt you and me. But it is our only hope, and the only way into the world we were made to live in. The only way to be who we were created to be. The only way to be free of Sin and Death.

In case it isn't already clear, this reckless love isn't license for us to do as we please. It is not OK for you and me to sin against one another, and against God. It is not OK for others to sin against us. That is not what reckless love means. As Paul says in Romans 'Shall we go on sinning, so that Grace may abound? By no means!' It is not license for us to do to each other as we please, without complaint, comment, or redress.

No - reckless love compels repentance and confession as a response to our own failings. Reckless love recognises that when we were still lost, Jesus came and died for us. Reckless love wins us over by making a once for all sacrifice before we even recognised that we needed it, let alone asked for it.
Reckless love invites us into a relationship where Sin and Death are beaten, and to pass on that reckless love to others. Reckless love invites us to live in a world where no more sacrifice is needed.

God has done it all. He has laid all his cards on the table. No more sacrifice is needed. How will you respond to this invitation into reckless love?

The Diamond of the Cross

The Powers Disarmed

Colossians 2:6-15
Guy Donegan-Cross. 7th October 2018

I was terrible at Geography at school. My 36% mark when I was 11 is burned into my brain. The pitiful look from my teacher. It made me feel like this amazing document the other day, in which the last two pages both said, 'This page is intentionally blank'. However, it's not a big deal - there are subjects it is OK not to be an expert at. On the other hand, this letter tells us that but there is one thing no human being can afford to be intentionally blank about. And this thing is so rich, so wonderful, so defining, that if we remain 'intentionally blank' about it, not only will we miss out, but we are more likely to be taken captive by endless arguments, empty traditions and superstitions.

By the way, Paul isn't arguing against philosophy, or thinking, or reason. He's not saying, 'Come to Jesus and turn your brain off.' He is just saying that true wisdom is to be found by studying the source of wisdom, and what He has done – fix your mind there.

We might like to think we can carry on as a blank page, but actually from day one of our lives we start making choices about our lives, our beliefs, our foundation which quickly direct the person we are becoming, how we live, and how we will ultimately respond to God, face to face.

And I'm saying that, in order to say this: that what we will explore today is not Christian baby food, but as he says elsewhere, 'meat' to chew on, and we have to be up for really digging in to what the cross means. In fact, it's the real centre of what the Bible teaches about what the cross means. I wonder if you can remember what the very first prophecy about Jesus was in Genesis? Or what the first thing the disciples said about Jesus was after Pentecost, when they had been entrusted with the message? Paul's words unpack that for us.

So the last thing Paul wants us to do is to be intentionally blank about what Jesus did on the cross, and this passage is like a revision course of all that we have been looking at...who Jesus is: the fullness of God – the totality of Him – how God, out of sheer love, takes the cross on Himself.

Who we are: those who have been given eternal life with him, symbolised through our dying and rising again in our baptism...this is amazing, but according to the Bible, it's not the main thing Jesus achieved on the cross.

Those who are forgiven, with everything we have ever done being wiped clean – no more guilt, shame or condemnation. No more proving ourselves through false religion. This is mind boggling, but it's not the main thing Jesus did for us.

Those who are marked with circumcision – thankfully not by human hands – but instead a mark which cannot be removed from us, and which shows that we are in an unbreakable and permanent covenant relationship of love with God, where we inherit all his salvation and authority to live...this is ground-shifting, but it's not the main thing.

So what is the main thing the cross is showing us? In a nutshell it is the climax of what God is working on throughout the whole of Scripture, from the beginning. The Bible is the story of God confronting cosmic, spiritual and human agents which seek to destroy, corrupt, and blight creation and human life at every level...these powers and authorities sometimes seen, sometimes unseen, which have used their God-given freedom, not to serve God, but to resist Him. Much like you and I have the freedom to do today. And on the cross, through the power of self-giving love, Jesus strips them of their power once and for all, showing them up for the sham they are – Paul uses the image of a defeated enemy being paraded through a city.

That's why the first Christians said this about Jesus. He is Christus Victor – he has overcome the enemy, and He is Lord. Without seeing this, we are unintentionally blank about the cross. To appreciate this, we need to see where the whole of Scripture is leading....

So what was the first prophecy about Him in Genesis? In fact, what's the first prophecy given in the Bible? Genesis 3:15 says that one day a descendant of Eve would be the one to crush the head of the serpent, the accuser, who had first brought the idea of rebellion into the world. This theme of conflict, and of there being spiritual forces at play, runs throughout the Bible. Frequently throughout the Old Testament God is portrayed as needing to do battle. Obviously, right from the beginning the satan is there in the garden. But it can be with unruly waters, which represent chaos, monsters such as the Leviathan in Job, which is so powerful that God can hardly contain it, hostile gods...many people in the Ancient Near Eastern world saw things through this lens – that there were real and threatening forces that come against God and need to be defeated, or contained.

In the Old Testament sometimes spiritual forces are seen behind every human battle. Elisha and his servant are surrounded by an earthly army and Elisha prays that his servant's eyes can be opened - and he looked and saw the hills full of horses and chariots of fire all around Elisha

In other words, the whole earth is not intentionally blank – it is not neutral territory – as CS Lewis put it, "There is no neutral ground in the universe. Every square inch, every split second is claimed by God, and counterclaimed by Satan.'

Did Jesus and his followers believe this? Jesus was accused by the Pharisees of using satan's power to drive out demons. Jesus, having said this is in effect, illogical, then says, '28 But if it is by the Spirit of God that I drive out demons, then the kingdom of God has come upon you.' In other words, when Jesus heals the sick and drives out evil spirits, satan's dominion is departing and God's kingdom is coming. In Luke, satan is depicted as the one who can offer Jesus all the kingdoms of the world if only he will worship him. Jesus calls him the 'prince of this world'. He talks about a woman who has been bound by satan for many years. He teaches us to pray, 'Deliver us from evil.'...what's going on? In Jesus' understanding, while God is the ultimate ruler, humans and spirits still have freedom to choose...and some behave as if God is not king – in the human world, but crucially in the heavenly world. So there is still a battle, and every time, for example, Jesus heals someone he is vanquishing evil, pushing it back. 'The thief comes only to steal, kill and destroy, but I have come that you might have life, and life in all its fullness.'

The world is not a blank page. And so after He had gone back to the Father, we see Jesus' disciples again and again proclaiming His victory over the powers of darkness. In the first great sermon of the church, Peter stands up at Pentecost to proclaim what Jesus has done. What does he say?

'This Jesus God raised up, and of that all of us are witnesses. Being therefore exalted at the right hand of God, and having received from the Father the promise of the Holy Spirit, he has poured out this that you both see and hear. For David did not ascend into the heavens, but he himself says, "The Lord said to my Lord, 'Sit at my right hand, until I make your enemies your footstool.'" Therefore let the entire house of Israel know with certainty that God has made him both Lord and Messiah, this Jesus whom you crucified.' (Acts 2:32-36)

The central thing about Jesus was that he had driven out God's enemies through the cross. In his first letter John says this: The reason the Son of God appeared was to destroy the devil's work. And in Hebrews we read that, 'he too shared in their humanity so that by his death he might break the power of him who holds the power of death—that is, the devil— 15 and free those who all their lives were held in slavery by their fear of death.'

In the Bible this world is not an intentionally blank page – there is no neutral territory, and there is no neutral life. Our biggest need to for evil to be driven out, and for God's kingdom of love to be established forever. If we don't see this we don't see the cross for what it means, and Jesus for who He is. Looking towards his death Jesus says, 'Now is the time for judgment on this world; now the prince of this world will be driven out.' The battle raging since the Garden will be decisively won.

Anyone who has read or seen the Narnia books will see this clearly. Aslan, the Jesus figure, comes to defeat the power of evil – White Witch, goblins – through the power of his own death – a power they cannot comprehend – and to restore the sons of Adam and daughters of Eve. So Paul writes that on the cross Jesus disarmed the powers, stripping all the spiritual tyrants in the universe of their sham authority at the Cross and marched them naked through the streets. The central message of the cross is Jesus is Lord, and he has won.

And this is so important to know, because we still await the final mopping up of these forces of evil. Despite their ultimate defeat, we still have a struggle against principalities and powers to fight. But they are sham – they have been humiliated. They do not have last word, or ultimate word, they can only accuse, suggest, or pretend.

Right from the moment you were baptised you acknowledged this central truth and you set out on a journey where Jesus is the Lord who has defeated the powers...Fight valiantly as a disciple of Christ against sin, the world and the devil, and remain faithful to Christ to the end of your life. May almighty God deliver you from the powers of darkness, restore in you the image of his glory, and lead you in the light and obedience of Christ.

Let's be canny, confident and courageous about this. In a couple of weeks it's Halloween. We don't celebrate it at St Mark's because while evil is a sham in many ways, we don't want to trivialise it either, or teach our kids to. Instead, we hold a light Party. We want to be canny about evil, knowing the world is not a blank page where it doesn't matter what you do, but territory where every heart, mind soul, part of creation can express light or darkness. So let's be canny and kick out darkness with light every chance we get.

In a few days I'm off to see U2 in Manchester. As part of their current show the lead singer Bono actually mocks the devil – a good principle. He pretends to be this stupid character called MacPhisto who rejoices in the rise of far-right hatred and the death of democracy...He ends his little mocking rant with a warning. 'It's when you don't believe I exist, that I do my best work.' We need to be canny, and alert. In my experience people who are canny about spiritual battle, like Jesus was, are good at doing two things – not blaming God for suffering, because they understand suffering as part of the battle, and not personalising conflicts with people. If you have fallen out with someone, or are in a difficult situation, Paul says not to see the person as the enemy. As far as you can, win the battle on your knees. Know that there is nothing the devil would like more than for you to make this child of God beside you into the problem. As Paul says in Ephesians, 'Don't give him a foothold.'

And we can be confident. The powers of darkness that blight the world are in their death throes. Death, sin, darkness, evil have had 'Time Up!' declared to them by the King of Kings and Lord of Lords. Because of His victory we have hope forever. I said earlier that 36% mark is still burned into my brain. Well, I don't particularly care, but some of us have shame that has burned itself into our hearts, or guilt, or definitions of ourselves that have stayed with us, and blighted us. In Colossians Paul says it's like an old arrest warrant cancelled and nailed to Christ's cross. The devil's name is the 'accuser' right from the beginning – a nagging, persistent reinforcement of our own unworthiness...

Well, Paul said, Christ not only blotted it clean, so that charge couldn't be read any more, but he nailed it to the cross – killed it, destroyed it. You can no longer be accused of being anything apart from His. And what's more, those spiritual tyrants who liked to pick it up, and shove it in your face, well, they were defeated, shamed and humiliated...Be confident it has been dealt with. When satan tempts you to despair, take that accusation, shove it in his face and say, 'This piece of paper is intentionally blank!'

The spiritual battle is one in which you cannot be a blank page. You must take sides. You get to follow in your daily life the one to whom every knee will bow. We can over-spiritualise the battle. Every time you bring light into the darkness – through acts of love, compassion, creativity, fostering, goodness done in Jesus' name you are following Him, and seeing His kingdom push out the kingdom of darkness. His love has already won – now we are cleaning up with him. My final c is confidence. Have confidence, soldiers of Christ, armed with love. Go forth into the world in peace; Be of good courage, Hold fast that which is good, Render to no one evil for evil. Strengthen the fainthearted, support the weak, Help the afflicted, Honour all persons. Love and serve the Lord, Rejoicing in the power of the Spirit, And the blessing of God the Father, Son, and the Holy Spirit be upon you and remain with you always. Amen.

The Diamond of the Cross

Slavery Ended

Romans 8:18-25
Neil Tunnicliffe. 21st October 2018

Brothers and sisters, you may find this difficult to believe – but I am middle-aged. I have come to this realisation through observation of a number of indicators: the fact that I can't stand up or sit down without making an involuntary noise; the amount of unwelcome hair that is sprouting from my nose and ears; the tendency of my wardrobe to shrink the waistbands of my trousers whenever I hang them up. The fact that I keep reminiscing about things I did when I was a teenager – and then remembering, that was as many as 35 years ago ...

I also find myself targeted by TV programmes and things on the internet which offer amusing retrospectives on how things used to be in the 1970s and 1980s. If you're on Facebook, you've probably seen things like this keep popping up. Do you remember playing with clackers in the schoolyard? Do you remember the pop lorry coming round, and offering you money to return your glass bottles? Do you remember having to put a pencil in a cassette to rewind the tape when it unravelled? Do you remember the Indoor League with Fred Trueman? That sort of thing.

There are also those TV programmes which remind us how awful television was in the 1970s – how racist and sexist and shocking it was, how they said things in those days that would be considered wholly unacceptable now. Shows like Love Thy Neighbour, It Ain't Half Hot Mum, Till Death Us Do Part, Are You Being Served – all of them using racism, sexism and homophobia as staples of their comedy, and which we didn't think anything of at the time. Very different days indeed.

Mind you, there was one TV programme in the 1970s which I remember vividly, and which had a profound effect not only on me as a youngster, but also on a large part of the Western world. It was called Roots: it was broadcast in 1977, and based on a novel by a black American called Alex Haley who had had strong associations with the civil rights movement in the USA in 1960s and 1970s.

Haley had traced his family history back to its origins in slavery in the 18th century, when his ancestor Kunta Kinte was forcibly abducted from the Gambia and taken across the Atlantic Ocean in chains to work on the plantations in Maryland. Roots was the story of Haley's family, and told in graphic detail what the lives of slaves were like in the 18th and 19th centuries, and the inhuman treatment they suffered at the hands of their owners, who were free to use and abuse them as they saw fit.

The casual brutality of the slavery portrayed in Roots was shocking to Western consciousness, especially those of us in my generation who were young enough to have been shielded from the truth that human beings sometimes treat each other in this barbaric manner. The impact it had was similar to that which was probably felt by those of you who are younger than me – which is an ever-increasing number of you – and who saw the more recent film 12 Years A Slave, which won an Oscar in 2013. It's probably not overdramatic to suggest that the reality presented by Roots gave significant impetus to the notion that a great and long-lasting injustice had been perpetrated through the slave trade, and that more – much more – now needed to be done to put right the wrongs of the past.

Nowadays when we talk about the slave trade, it's this kind of thing that we have in mind – the awful traffic between Africa and the Americas, and the hideous conditions imposed on those working in the plantations of the Deep South and the West Indies. But in truth, there was nothing new in this trade. Slavery is as old as man himself, and was one of the identifying features of the society that Paul was a member of, and into which he wrote the letter which we are looking at this morning.

The context for Paul's letter to the Romans was this. Around the turn of the first century AD, between 30 and 40 per cent of the population of Italy were slaves. This meant a total of between 2 and 3 million people by the time of Jesus's birth – and so every third person you met in Italy, in Rome, was a slave. This was the peak period for slavery under the Roman Empire: it was the time when the boundaries of empire were extended dramatically through a series of wars in the East, in the West, and to the North. And successful wars brought slaves. Rome's military policy was harsh and oppressive: if you chose to fight against her, and you lost, then your fate was either death or slavery. And so the more successful wars Rome fought, the more slaves she had.

By contrast with America in the 18th and 19th centuries, Rome's slaves were not defined by race. The wars fought by Rome meant that its slaves came from all over Europe and the Mediterranean: France, Spain, Germany, Britain, North Africa, the Balkans, Greece, Asia Minor – even from Israel itself. A vivid example of this is the Jewish Revolt in the late 60s AD, the one that led to the destruction of the temple in Jerusalem in 70 AD that was foretold by Jesus in the Gospels. The Jewish historian Josephus tells us that, after the Romans took the city and slaughtered all the men who were under arms and the aged and infirm, they sold into slavery all the rest. This was a total of 97,000 people – more than the population of Harrogate and Knaresborough combined.

Life for a slave in Rome was little different from that depicted in Roots or in 12 Years A Slave. Under Roman law slaves were considered to be no more than useful bodies, no more than property. They were bodies that were put to work. They were entirely at the mercy and disposal of their masters – some of whom were good, others not so good. They could be subjected to corporal punishment, sexual exploitation (prostitutes were often slaves), torture, and summary execution. Unlike Roman citizens, slaves had no legal identity or rights: they could not own property, their testimony could not be accepted in a court of law. In effect, they were non-people.

One of the consequences of this was that the life expectancy of a slave in the city of Rome was extraordinarily low: just 17.5 years on average. By comparison, life expectancy of the citizen population as a whole was much higher: if they made it through childhood and its risk of disease, a third of free people would make it into their 60s, while the overall average was in the mid-20s.

The one abiding hope of all slaves was for manumission – that is, to be set free by their owners. Slaves could be freed for a variety of reasons; distinguished service, a particularly good deed toward the slave's owner, or out of friendship or respect. Sometimes, a slave who had enough money could buy his freedom or that of a fellow slave – but few slaves had the money to do so, and most were not allowed to hold money. In any case, the law in the first century AD was that no slave could be freed before the age of 30 – and, given that their average life expectancy was just 17.5 years, the prospect of living long enough to earn your freedom was pretty small.

Slaves who were awarded their freedom received it together with the patronage of their former owner. The terms of the deal were that the slave was expected to support his former owner, his patron, as required in public life – e.g., by voting for them in elections – while the patron was expected to ensure a certain degree of material security for their former slaves. The deal could also involve the patron giving their name to the slave – which was a form of adoption into their extended family.

Why am I telling you all this? It's because the church in Rome to whom Paul was writing this letter in the mid-first century AD was comprised to a large extent of slaves. How do we know that? Well, from archaeological evidence including the catacombs underneath Rome that some of you might have visited while on holiday. And from history: the fact that, when the Emperor Nero persecuted the Christian church in the mid-60s AD, he was able to execute Christians in the most horrible ways – crucifixion, burning them alive, throwing them to wild animals in the arena – which simply would not have been allowed if those Christians had been Roman citizens. Also from sheer probability, given that – as we've already said – every third person in Rome at the time was a slave.

We can also infer it from the fact that, in chapter 6 of this letter, Paul uses two examples from contemporary life to illustrate what he is saying about the positive and negative things that bind us. One is marriage – and the other is slavery. (Insert your own punchline from the 1970s here ...) But these were both examples which he expected his audience to be able to relate to – and so this adds to the thesis that the church in Rome contained a large number of slaves.

So: Paul writes his letter to the Romans to a community of genuine, actual slaves. People who were a possession, and who were liable at any moment to be beaten, abused or executed for little or no reason. People who once had something, and now had nothing – no property, no identity, no rights, no control over their own bodies: nothing. People who were a long way from home, forcibly separated from their families and relatives, many of whom were likely to have been killed by their captors. People who were desperate in the literal meaning of the word, which is to say that they were entirely without hope. Except for this one hope that, by some distant and unlikely event, they might be set free.

Knowing this can – and should – transform the way that we read the letter to the Romans. Especially the way that Paul uses slavery as a motif, as a metaphor, for the issues that he's looking to unpack. One of Paul's abiding themes in this letter – and it's a complex letter, not necessarily one that can be reduced to a single summary phrase – is the way we are bound by, constrained by, held in slavery by sin; but also that, if we seek to replace that by a slavish observation of the Laws of the Old Testament, we are no less held in slavery. Only through faith in God, and a life lived in and through the Holy Spirit, can we be liberated from all these constraints. Only that represents true freedom.

I think we can only truly understand this motif, this concept of a process of liberation into freedom, this idea of redemption, if we first understand slavery. If we understand what it meant – and means – to be a slave. The place that slaves came from, the experiences which they had had, the conditions in which they lived. Knowing all of that should help to give us a right reading of this letter, and all that is in it.

In chapter 8 Paul talks about the people suffering and groaning inwardly as they eagerly await the arrival of this freedom, the redemption of their bodies and their adoption as sons. What is significant here is that the language he uses is technical: the Greek words he chooses are legal ones. They relate to the process of someone buying someone else out of slavery, and to their formal adoption into the extended family of a patron. Given the profile of the Roman church of the time, these terms would have been hugely emotive. The currency which they would have had with Paul's Roman audience was enormous. Together, they defined everything that slaves in Rome were longing for, things they ate their hearts out for – but were unlikely ever to achieve.

By using these words, Paul is tapping into the only real hope that this audience had – a hope that may have been slim, hardly a hope at all, but one that was none the less urgent and fervent.

These people longed to be set free from their bondage. They longed to be given their rights back, to be recognised as a real person. They longed to have a house, a family, of their own again. They longed to have a name again, and the practical support of the one who had given them it.

So when Paul talks about redemption, the offer he's holding out to these people – that faith in God and a life lived in and through the Holy Spirit is freedom – addresses their deepest needs and desires. OK, maybe not physically, and maybe not in the here and now: the weight of hundreds of years of human history, and the power of Rome, stand against that. But the good news that Paul is proclaiming is that, somehow, if not in this life then in the next one, the things these people long for will be theirs. They will be bought out of slavery. They will be free. They will have identity, and rights, and personhood. They will have the support of a patron who loves them and looks after them – the patronage of the one true God. They will have a family again – the family of the children of God.

I think that in the 21st century we have lost the power of this passage. We have developed a tendency to read Paul's letter to the Romans as a work of philosophy, of metaphor. To believe that it refers merely to man's metaphorical slavery to our appetites, and to death. That the redemption of our bodies signals freedom from our physical wants and needs, and from the unfortunate tendency of our body to decline and decay – much like my own in middle age. And that this will only fully apply when we die or when the Kingdom comes.

And we look at this, and we think: well that's nice, isn't it? That's OK. I'm pretty comfortable now, except for the odd ache and pain – and so the good news is reduced to a promise that those aches and pains will be gone when we come into the Kingdom. And so the freedom, the new life, the radical transformation that is ahead of us – the glory that will be revealed in us, in Paul's words – is diminished to a mild sense of relief that, when the

Kingdom comes, we won't be bothered by hunger or indigestion, and we'll have new bodies that won't have arthritis, or bunions, or short-sightedness, or be slightly deaf in one ear.

I think the challenge for us, with all our 21st century comforts, our wealth and our privilege, is this. How can we share the urgency and fervency with which the church in Rome received Paul's offer of freedom? How can we ensure that we approach this prospect of redemption and adoption with the same desperate longing that the slaves in Rome must have felt? How can we come into empathy, a full appreciation of the sheer scale of the hope that is embodied in this passage?

To do this, I think we have to build our own vision of slavery in the world today, and to recognise our own place in this. I don't just mean acknowledging that slavery still exists in the 21st century – although of course it does, albeit at levels much lower than the 30 or 40 per cent of society that pertained in Italy in Paul's day. And of course it's right and important to recognise this, and to try to put ourselves in the shoes of these people, to see through their eyes, to understand the terrible circumstances of war or inequality or societal norms or economic desperation which have led to their enslavement, and to campaign for, to work for their release as a manifestation of God's Kingdom.

But we can also broaden our vision of slavery by recognising the warfare that enslaves people within our immediate vicinity, even here in leafy Harrogate. I'm talking here about the battlegrounds that exist for people's health, happiness and wellbeing; about the negative experiences, behaviours, desires and habits that people fight against, and lose. And so they become captive to bitterness or regret after a failed relationship, or a personal conflict, or a business that has folded, or a redundancy. Or they are trapped by mental health issues, depression, despair and suicidal thoughts. Or they are unable to escape from their own low self-esteem, or the inflexible opinions of others – the disapproval or disappointment of a parent; or they live in fear of what the future brings, or of being let down. Or they are crippled by bereavement, the loss of a loved one, and their inability to move on. Or they are bound by a drive to gather more and more material wealth, either to keep up with the Joneses, or because they crave the security that they think it brings. Or they are addicts in various ways, be it to substance abuse or unhealthy habits.

This new vision, this redefinition of slavery brings a much higher percentage of people into its orbit – maybe even more than the 30 or 40 per cent of society that Paul knew. Maybe this definition includes you and me. I don't want to be presumptuous, but I think most of us would say that we have been taken captive and enslaved at some stage by something in our lives – whether it's one of the things that I've just listed, or some other thing that only you know. And all these are forms of slavery carry their own quiet desperation – but the good news of Paul's letter to the Romans is that God wants to redeem you and me, to liberate us from that slavery; to allow us to live a life under His patronage that is free in every sense of the word.

We also have to recognise what hangs on this redemption – what Paul says will be triggered by it, follow on from it as a necessary consequence. Here in chapter 8 Paul says that, in the same way that those humans who are living in slavery are groaning under the weight of the suffering that they bear, longing to be freed from it, so is creation. There is hope, however, that creation can be liberated from its bondage to decay and brought into the same freedom that faith in God and life in the Spirit will bring to mankind.

Paul's words here are often construed as a green manifesto: a statement that creation's decline and decay is to a large extent linked to our own moral and spiritual decline, and that our response should be to wise up and be better stewards of it. And that's OK: if these verses lead us to look after the planet with a little more care and attention, then all well and good. But I think that interpretation provides too narrow a reading of Paul's words, and it limits, it misses the full width and breadth, the full glory, of what Paul is talking about.

For one thing, the word that Paul uses that we translate as 'creation', a more accurate rendering of it would be 'the universe and everything that is in it'. Paul isn't just talking about the way that we manage our lands and oceans. He's talking about everything that is and has been made by God: not only the earth, but the planets, the stars, the galaxies, the universes beyond. He's talking about life in all its forms, from the sub-atomic level to the gigantic and colossal, from single-cell amoebas to the most complex life forms. He's talking about all matter and energy, all time and space. He's talking about everything that God has conceived, whether within our perception or not.

And the suffering, the longing, that this creation in its fullest sense is labouring under is markedly different to that of mankind. Paul says that creation's groaning is not like ours: its longing is to give birth, to be fruitful, in a way that has been frustrated. Trapped in a repeating cycle of decay and death, it is a poor imitation of what it might be. Creation is empty, vain, lacking in meaning or purpose, fruitless, idle, folly – all of which are viable translations of the word in verse 20 which is conveyed in the NIV as 'subject to frustration'. But when God's Kingdom comes – when slavery is ended, redemption comes about, and all people are restored to God's family – then creation will respond with its own redemption and renewal, and bear fruit like never before. According to Paul, this fruitfulness will come after, and as a consequence of, the sons of God being revealed – and this is what creation is waiting for. The whole universe is waiting for this revelation – for God's Kingdom to come, for mankind to be rid of slavery in all its forms, for us to be redeemed and to enter into God's family – because this will be the sign for creation also to share our freedom.

What will that look like? I simply don't know – and neither did Paul! But it sounds pretty good, doesn't it? The vital powers of the universe freed and unleashed, and working in harmony with God's purposes. All the wonders and marvels of nature unchained and able to burst forth in a riot of creative beauty. No longer constrained by decay and death, but blossoming and flowering in ways that are fruitful and sustainable. No longer bound by the need for consumption, and food chains, and dog eating dog: as it's promised in Isaiah chapter 11, the wolf lying down with the lamb, the leopard with the goat, the lion eating straw with the ox, young children playing near the cobra and putting their hands in viper's nests. The whole earth – the whole universe – full of the knowledge of the Lord as the waters cover the sea.

Isn't that something worth hoping for – worth longing for? Doesn't that make us appreciate the sheer scale, the size of the offer that God is making us? Doesn't that bring us somewhere close to the feeling that the slaves of Rome must have had when they contemplated Paul's words? When Paul talks about the glory that will be revealed in us, this is what he is talking about: not just a new body with no bunions and 20:20 vision – but the restoration, the redemption of all things, an end to slavery in all its forms, and adoption into the worldwide family of God. Not just a new earth, but a new heaven too, a universe which functions solely for life and no longer for death. The peace of God, which passes all understanding. And a world without end, Amen.

So what have we said this morning? In summary, it's that we cannot begin to understand redemption until we first understand slavery. And slavery comes in so many forms that, even now in the 21st century, most if not all of us will be able to identify something which either has held, or does still hold us in captivity. And so we should approach the promise of God's redemption with the same longing and desperation that the slaves in Rome two thousand years ago would have felt. And we should work urgently and passionately to bring that redemption about, in our own lives and in the lives of others, in the promise that – when it comes – it will completely transform everything in our world. My prayer for you this morning/afternoon is this: may you come to a full recognition and appreciation of the power and urgency of Paul's words in these verses that we have read today. May you long for the coming of God's Kingdom with the longing that a slave feels for his freedom. May you long to be part of that Kingdom with the longing that the displaced, the refugees, the prisoners-of-war feel for their home and their family. May you recognise all that hangs on the coming of God's Kingdom – the full extent of the glory that is at stake, the restoration of the universe and all that is in it to a state of balance and harmony with God's purpose. May it be your fervent prayer, and may you act every day, to bring that Kingdom on. In Jesus's holy name, Amen.

The Diamond of the Cross

True Power

Philippians 2:5-8
Guy Donegan-Cross. 4th November 2018

If I asked you, 'Who is the most powerful person in the world today?', you would probably respond: Trump, Putin etc.

And this would be how most people think. From when we are young having power means being able to tell others what to do. Parents, teachers, employers. Strong governments are those who can tell others what to do, and put themselves first.

And we can grow up thinking that we should be like that. We should come out on top. We should be recognised. We should be strongest. Because that's what power is like.

A lot of people also think that is what God should be like. He is so powerful He can do whatever He wants. And that is partly true. If He wanted, God could make everyone obey Him.

But if God is like that then that raises at least two questions.

If God is so powerful why doesn't He just intervene and sort everything out?
And if God is so powerful then how can I choose not to do what He wants?

Because God's power is the opposite of what you expect. He doesn't control you. He doesn't manipulate you. He doesn't coerce you.

Instead, he serves you.

Jesus said, 'The Son of Man came not to be served, but to serve, and to give up His life.'

This is the strangest thing to get our heads around. But it's also the most wonderful truth about how beautiful, kind, and overwhelming the love and character of God is.

This little section is one of the earliest bits of writing we have about how the early Christians understood Jesus. And so it's one of the most important ways we get to see into the heart of God.

And what we find is this:

God doesn't do power like we do power. In fact he does the opposite.

Jesus had equal status with God – you might expect Him to show us how powerful He is. But He doesn't. He becomes a slave.
Jesus could have called millions of angels to help Him. But He didn't. He let soldiers pierce His hands and feet.
Jesus could have been the biggest Someone the world had ever seen. But He didn't. He became nothing.
Jesus could have forced everyone to obey Him. But he didn't. He became obedient.

This is true power. It's the power of emptying yourself. And that is God's heart. To empty Himself, for the sake of others.

I don't love God because He controls everything, sorts everything out, looks stronger than anyone else.

I love God because His essence is humility. It looks weak, and broken, and lost in the short term. But it's a power that overcomes evil with love, because evil can't understand it or defeat it. Wouldn't you want to worship a God like that?

If I asked you, 'Whose use of power in the world looks most like Jesus?' You might have a different answer.

You might say Mother Theresa, who said, "If you are humble nothing will touch you, neither praise nor disgrace, because you know what you are.'

You might say Mary, who said, "Behold the handmaid of the Lord. Be it done unto me according to your word.' (Luke 1:38)

I don't expect it will be people who make the headlines.

Paul said, 'Have the same mindset as Jesus...who became a slave.'

The best material to send to the future is humility. But this can be really hard for us.

Once Muhammad Ali was flying to one of his engagements. During the flight the aircraft ran into foul weather, and mild to moderate turbulence began to toss it about. The passengers were accordingly instructed to fasten their seatbelts immediately. Everyone complied but Ali. Noticing this, the flight attendant approached him and requested that he observe the captain's order, only to hear Ali audaciously respond, 'Superman don't need no seatbelt.' The flight attendant did not miss a beat and replied, 'Superman don't need no airplane either.'

The world teaches us one version of power. And it can be really hard to kick this. Unless we look at the cross, and fall in love with the God whose power is made perfect in weakness.

Because as we do that we realise that true power is all about emptying ourselves.

In Vienna there is a church in which the deceased members of the former ruling family in Austria, the Hapsburgs, are buried. When the royal funeral processions arrived at the church, the mourners would knock at the door and ask to be allowed in. A priest inside would reply, 'Who is it that desires admission here?' The mourners would call out, 'His apostolic majesty, the emperor.' The priest would then answer, 'I don't know him.' Then the mourners would knock a second time, and the priest would again ask who was there. The mourners would repeat, 'The highest emperor.' When this happened a third time, the priest would ask, 'Who is it?' The third time the answer would be, 'A poor sinner, your brother' -- and the funeral procession would be allowed to enter.'

Appetite says, 'Be sensuous, enjoy yourself.'
Education says, 'Be resourceful, expand yourself.'
Materialism says, 'Be satisfied, please yourself.'
Psychology says, 'Be confident, fulfil yourself.'
Humanism says, 'Be capable, believe in yourself.'
Pride says, 'Be superior, promote yourself.'
Jesus says, 'Be wise, humble yourself.'

What do those we mentioned at the end have in common? Mother Theresa, Martin Luther King, Mark, John Wesley, Corrie ten Boom, Oscar Romero, Teresa of Avila, Dietrich Bonhoeffer, Saint Francis of Assissi, Asia Bibbi? They all emptied themselves for Christ.

And they changed the world.

I came across a litany the other day that expresses the heart of a humble person.

That others may be loved more than I,
Jesus, grant me the grace to desire it.
That others may be chosen and I set aside,
Jesus, grant me the grace to desire it.
That others may be praised and I go unnoticed,
Jesus, grant me the grace to desire it.

It may be hard to pray, but only when we all live like this, will the world get healed.

So to finish, how do you know if your heart is moving towards the self-emptying love of God or not? Can I suggest two questions as litmus tests:

Do you remain teachable?

Can you pass on praise to God?

The Diamond of the Cross

God has No Split Personality
2 Corinthians 5:11-21
Kim Mason. 18th November 2018

Adam is a workaholic.
Up at 6am, working a 13hr day in a successful job where he is
climbing the ranks of senior leadership. He will make partner
before the end of his career, but
He is increasingly estranged from his family. His children and
wife feel like constant disappointments to him as he sets
ridiculously high bars for the personal achievement and public
appearance.

He perceives that everything in his life is being judged; his work,
clothes, car, the behaviour of his kids, the presentation of his
house.

He needs to prove his sense of worth and value because he has
this niggling sense of disapproval, anger perhaps, at the back of
his mind and he needs to placate it...

Hold Adam in your mind for later...

After having spent nearly a whole year thinking about the action
of the cross, and what and how it achieves it, I hope you have
come to see that the Bible doesn't give us a definitive, one
perfect way to understand the cross. Instead we have a plethora
of images and metaphors and messages about what the cross
does for our relationship with God and how it does it. And the
image we find here in 2 Corinthians 5:11-21 is of reconciliation.

There are three elements that I want to draw out of this passage
this morning, about God, about us, and about the world.

ABOUT GOD

'[...] God, [...] reconciled us to himself through Christ and gave us the ministry of reconciliation: that God was reconciling the world to himself in Christ, not counting people's sins against them. And he has committed to us the message of reconciliation.' (2 Corinthians 5:18-19)

I wonder what mental picture you have in your mind when you think of the moment of Jesus crucifixion? God the Son is clearly on the cross, but where is God the Father? Or God the Holy Spirit? Are they a part of that image too?

Sometimes we can be confused into thinking that God the Father is distant up in heaven emanating anger and wrath towards a vulnerable and servant hearted Jesus pinned on the cross. The Father is angry at Jesus, anger that should have been directed at us. At our failure Our lack, shortfall Our not good enough-ness. Anger now thankfully redirected at Jesus, and away from us.

Songs like, In Christ Alone perpetuate this idea of the anger or wrath of God. In the second verse we sing:

> 'Til on that cross as Jesus died,
> The wrath of God was satisfied

The Father is angry at us, and Jesus is soaking up the anger and the punishment on our behalf.

I wonder if that rings true with your image of the cross.
Well I hope not, because it couldn't be further from the truth.

2 Corinthians tells us that God was IN Christ on the cross
The whole of God, the Trinity, was in Christ on the cross

That is the beauty of the Trinity, three for the price of one.

God is one - it is a fundamental doctrine of the Jewish and
Christian faiths
One God, unified in thought and word and deed
There is no sense in which the Father's will, thoughts or actions
can be separated from the Son's will, thought and actions

So if we have any image of the cross which separates the Trinity
and has them thinking or feeling differently about it, then that's
not a true image of the cross.

Christ wasn't out on a limb, doing his own thing on the cross
The fullness of God was in Christ on the cross

That means that when we look at the cross and see the arms of
Jesus outstretched in love
We also look and see the embrace of the Father, like the prodigal
Father
Waiting for us, reaching out for us, embracing us in love.

The real danger in talking of Jesus satisfying God's wrath is that
we separate the actions of the Trinity in the cross. It appears to
portray loving Jesus saving us from an angry God who metes out
his punishment upon the innocent. Instead, we should see in the
open arms of Jesus a welcome by a loving Father, who no longer
counts our sin against us—it is from our sin and its
consequences that Jesus saves us, rather than from a hateful
God.

The second thing I want to draw out of this passage is what it
tells us about us.

If God is in Christ on the cross, reconciling us to himself
The possibility for the wrath of God
Being directed at Jesus, or at us
Is removed

God is not angry with us

God's demeanour towards us is always one of love

Think back to Adam
Always trying to perform
Always trying to be perfect
Always trying to guard against any sense of disapproval or anger

A faithful Christian disciple / mature
And yet in the ground of his being, at some fundamental level, he
is trying to appease his maker.
Trying to avoid the wrath of God.

But what he doesn't understand is the wrath of God has never
been directed at him
At me, at you
The wrath of God is solely reserved for evil and sin
For the sin that so easily entangles us, but never for us

Eugene Peterson the author of The Message translation of the
Bible, died this year. In his eulogy, his son said Eugene only ever
had one sermon, one message:
'God loves you. He's on your side. He's coming after you. He's
relentless.'

In his love, God has reconciled us to himself
Reconciliation is the restoration of friendship
God was reconciling us to himself for friendship. In love.

So the cross functions to close the gap between us and God

Sin separates us from God
Jesus bears the consequence of our sin - the separation from God
So that we can be reconciled to God
Instead of being separated
We are close. We are friends

THE WORLD

'Therefore, if anyone is in Christ, the new creation has come: The old has gone, the new is here! All this is from God, who reconciled us to himself through Christ and gave us the ministry of reconciliation: that God was reconciling the world to himself in Christ, not counting people's sins against them. And he has committed to us the message of reconciliation. We are therefore Christ's ambassadors, as though God were making his appeal through us. We implore you on Christ's behalf: Be reconciled to God.' (2 Corinthians 5:17-20)

Paul calls us to step into a ministry of reconciliation.
A ministry of mending broken relationships in the world.
A ministry of restoring friendship.

Reconciliation between
People and God   God's not angry
and judging
People and themselves   self-acceptance
People and other people   family
People and creation   harmony

Verse 20 is fascinating
> 'We are therefore Christ's ambassadors, as though God were making his appeal through us. We implore you on Christ's behalf: Be reconciled to God.' (2 Corinthians 5:20)

God is proclaiming his good news through our lives. He is making his appeal through our lives; how people see us and perceive us. It is the visibility of our lives that makes us ambassadors.

And so Paul exhorts us to be reconciled to God

And that is because it is possible to live as Christians, as the Corinthians were doing, without sharing in reconciliation, either with others or with ourselves and occasionally with God.

And yet if we don't step into that reconciliation, what are we being ambassadors of?

We are called to be Christ's ambassadors in the world. We are a sent people. The way people experience us living our lives is the gospel. But we need to be a healed and reconciled people too.

The Diamond of the Cross

It's Personal

Galatians 2:15-21
Michelle Lepine. 25th November 2018

Sometimes when something is wrong, it needs to be put right.

In 1995 the Truth and Reconciliation Commission was established in South Africa in order to carry out an inquiry into the apartheid-related atrocities and crimes committed by the White dominated government against the Black majority. Whilst opinions were divided regarding the appropriate action to take, the inquiry's aim also focussed on ways in which to unite and rebuild the nation. Some people wanted harsh penalties for the perpetrators of the crimes, whilst others preferred to simply forget the whole thing.

I wonder do we sometimes apply the same approach to our relationship with God ? Paul talks about this when he writes about 'justification' by which he means 'being made right with God.' I suspect that for many of us, Christians and non-Christians alike, our first thoughts about putting right our relationship with God might turn to the idea of having to do something quite spectacular in order to earn the right. This is a way of thinking that is typical of the world in which we live. We are told that there's no such thing as a free lunch and if something is too good to be true, then it usually means that it is. Let's put it another way, if I have done something to hurt someone, my first thoughts centre around what I can do to make things right with them again, similar to the example of the Truth & Reconciliation Committee in South Africa..

This was indeed the way that some of the early Jewish Christians also thought as we see in this passage from Galatians. They thought that Justification or being made right with God could only happen by a strict application of the law. In other words, by the outward signs of their obedience to religious practices such as circumcision and only eating with other fellow Jewish Christians who shared their practices.

But Paul reminds them and us that this is not the case. In verse 16 he writes, 'we have come to believe in Christ Jesus, so that we might be justified by faith in Christ, and not by doing the works of the law.' This was not the message they expected to hear and yet it's a message that reflects the very heart of the gospel; that our relationship with Jesus is one of love. In fact so important is it that Paul repeats it 3 times in verse 16 alone. I get the impression that Paul wanted us to really take it on board!

Paul wants us to know that faith in Jesus alone is the key to our relationship with God. His point is that to think that we can earn justification is somehow to undermine the fundamental role of faith. Faith is key.

But what do we mean when we talk about faith? Paul suggests that the faith that he is talking about in Galatians can take on two meanings. Firstly our faith in Jesus. That means more than simply believing in Jesus but rather implies acknowledging his sovereignty over all aspects of our lives. It means relinquishing control and trusting in him. In verse 20 Paul talks about being 'crucified with Christ' – 'I have been crucified with Christ and I no longer live, but Christ lives in me.' I think this is what Paul means when he says these words.

It's about giving our all to him, making ourselves totally dependent on him and allowing him to govern and guide every aspect of who we are and how we think and live. It implies a faith that is demanding and sacrificial at all costs. In other words it's a call to surrender ourselves to Jesus. For some of us, myself included, that can feel uncomfortable.

Well perhaps Paul's second definition of faith can help. He writes also about the faith of Jesus; a meaning that is implied in the original Greek. It's a subtle change but the affect it has on our understanding and subsequent response is important: firstly it takes away the idea of anything that we do to earn it, since our being made right with God is not dependent on the purity or strength of our own faith (thankfully!). It 's not about us. Rather we are justified through the unfaltering, incomparable faith of Jesus – his faithfulness in obedience to the Father, his surrender to the will of God and for the sake of humanity as manifested in his self-sacrificial death on the cross. Christ died for me, therefore I give my life to Christ.

Our faith in Jesus is strengthened as a result of the faith of Jesus and demands nothing less than to allow ourselves to be amazed, either for the first time or once again at God's incomprehensible love for us and the selfless action of Jesus. And through our amazement at his love for us be compelled to give our very all to him for all that he has done for us.

Perhaps Isaac Watts came somewhere close when he wrote the following lyrics to the well-known hymn:
> *Love so amazing, so divine,*
> *Demands my soul, my life, my all.*

To this end, what Paul is saying is that Jesus' death on the cross is personal.
In verses 19-21 Paul could not make this any more clear to us. The verses read as a personal statement of faith from Paul since he shifts from talking about 'we' to 'I' and I don't doubt that Paul wholeheartedly means every word. However, his intention is also to offer them as an invitation to us to enter into the same attitude of heart and to make the same statements of faith as he does - in other words to acknowledge and proclaim: Jesus died for me !

When something is personal it means that it touches you at the very core of your being and you cannot help but respond to it and be transformed by it. I remember saying 'It's personal' in 2014 when I undertook a major sporting challenge for Alzheimer's Society, a charity very close to my heart. My dad was in hospital at the time and dying of Alzheimer's. I had done quite a few races before but this one really mattered. I wasn't running it for myself or my own personal gain, I was doing it in honour of my dad ; to make his death count for something and out of gratitude for the love that he had afforded me throughout my life. That it was personal gave added impetus to the way that I thought about it, approached it and spoke about it with others. I gave it my very all.

When something is personal it adds a different meaning and takes us to a level that we could never before have imagined. It enhances the importance or urgency of something. But, it also adds accountability to us as individuals, often demands more commitment or sacrifice from us and a deeper personal response. It has a long lasting effect on us and it transforms us in some way.

So Jesus' death on the cross for me and you personally is not something that happened and is simply gratefully remembered, but rather it determines and shapes our everyday attitudes, values and practices now, today and tomorrow. It touches us at the very core of our being and we cannot help but to respond to it in faith and be transformed by it.

But what does that look like for us in reality?

The reality is that for many of us, and for various reasons, believing that Jesus died for us personally is a message that is difficult to comprehend and unreservedly believe.

Perhaps you are one of those people who struggles with the message that Jesus died for you. Perhaps because you don't feel good enough, or because your idea of God cannot comprehend such incomparable love and grace, or because your natural response is to strive for acceptance and for a place in God's Kingdom. Do you beat yourself up in prayer, feeling guilty, comparing yourself to others or needing to justify yourself before God? If that's you then you haven't grasped that your relationship with Jesus is one of love. If that's you, then it might mean simply taking that first step to knowing and being willing to accept the outpouring of Jesus's love and grace on the cross for you. It's a first step towards letting go of the control you want to have on your own life and surrendering yourself to God.

The late Evangelist Billy Graham pointed out:

'God proved His love on the cross. When Christ hung, and bled, and died, it was God saying to the world "I love you."'

On the other hand, perhaps you are someone who thinks that you never do anything wrong. Are you someone who holds a grudge, judges others or sometimes lacks humility? If that's you, then you haven't grasped that your relationship with Jesus is one of love.

As Chair of the Truth and Reconciliation Commission mentioned earlier, Desmond Tutu took a different approach to putting things right in South Africa. He promoted a culture of forgiveness in order to heal emotions and wounds of anger and hatred with a view to achieving reconciliation. Tutu said he 'witnessed so many incredible people, who despite experiencing atrocity and tragedy have come to a point in their lives where they are able to forgive,' one of them being a teenage daughter of a victim ambushed and killed in a car fire in 1984.

Paul said : '...I live by faith in the Son of God, who loved me and gave himself for me.'

For many of us it may simply be a reminder to trust more and to surrender more of ourselves to God. To put ourselves completely in God's hands in such a way that the words 'I no longer live, but Christ lives in me' might become an actual reality in the way we each live, think, act, share and give.

Many of you will be familiar with the story of Jackie Pullinger, who as a young adult in the 1960s, felt called to go to Hong Kong after a dream. After being turned down by a number of Missionary Societies, she asked the advice of a vicar in Shoreditch, who told her that she should just go, if God was telling her to. His advice to her was: 'If you had a job, a ticket, accommodation, a sick fund and a pension, you wouldn't need to trust Him. If I were you I would go out and buy a ticket for a boat going on the longest journey you can find and pray to know where to get off... You can't lose if you put yourself completely in God's hands, you know.'

And so Jackie did just that and her work in the infamous, dark 'Walled City' led to thousands of people being set free from addiction by faith in Jesus and they continue to do so today.

Your relationship with Jesus is one of love. Are you prepared to be reconciled to God in the Christ-centred way that Desmond Tutu promoted? Or to 'put yourself completely in God's hands' like Jackie Pullinger and surrender in faith to the one who gave up everything for you?

The Life of The Cross

Freedom!
The ABC of God Confidence
Baptised into Christ
We have this Ministry
Where true Strength comes from

The Life of The Cross

Freedom!

Romans 8:1-17
Guy Donegan-Cross. 7th January 2019

What shape is your life? By which I mean, what is your life identified most with as its foundation? Is it pound shaped? Zero shaped? Paul said, 'I have been crucified with Christ.' In other words, I identify completely with everything that happened on the cross. Everything the cross is about applies to me, and from now on it shapes my choices, my thoughts, my identity, my feelings, my relationship with God.

Over the next few weeks, we look at the characteristics of cross-shaped people. What do our lives look like? How do we feel inside? What difference does it make? And today the starting point is this. If you are cross-shaped you will be most characterised by freedom and joy!

Do you want freedom? In your lived experience? True freedom? The freedom that Jesus meant when he said, 'If the Son sets you free, you shall be free indeed?' The freedom that Paul, the 'apostle of freedom' was talking about when he said, 'we have been released from the law so that we serve in the new way of the Spirit'? Or when he said, 'Thanks be to God, who delivers me through Jesus Christ our Lord!' Or when he declared, '...there is now no condemnation for those who are in Christ Jesus, because through Christ Jesus the law of the Spirit who gives life has set you free from the law of sin and death....The Spirit you received does not make you slaves, so that you live in fear again...'?

Do you want to be truly free? Because I am sure when God looks at us he wants us to enjoy what Paul calls 'the glorious freedom of the children of God.'

The whole point of the good news is freedom. The cross brings freedom. And precisely how that happens and is lived out is unpacked here in this letter.

But to be truly free we must understand the inadequacy of the freedom that is sold to us. It is a cheap imitation of freedom.

If you are a fan of the Primal Scream album 'Screamadelica' you will have a heard a classic expression of hedonistic freedom.

Just what is it that you want to do?
We wanna be free
We wanna be free to do what we wanna do
And we wanna get loaded
And we wanna have a good time

It captured a mood that said freedom is about doing what we want to do and being who we want to be.

For people in our culture freedom of expression is the primary freedom, even the
primary point of life. If I can live life how I want it that is what matters.

While it's good to open, honest and authentic, and to have parties, there are so many problems with this as a philosophy of life, and a definition of freedom, it's hard to know where to begin...

If you don't believe in God, for example, your freedom is pretty much at the mercy of your genes – what you experience as freedom is more an expression of your genetic makeup than anything else.
You'll probably find that your freedom to express yourself becomes pretty quickly affected by life circumstances you can't

control – the amount of money you have, or your health, for example.

And it's amazing how in this supposedly tolerant and non-judgmental climate the internet can come down like a ton of bricks on anyone whose opinion does not conform.

This kind of freedom is really an illusion and can tend towards being very narcissistic.

True, human, deep, eternal freedom is so much more than the ability to self-express. Paul describes it the glorious freedom of the children of God. It is less about knowing who you are, and more about knowing whose you are. The aim of freedom is not to be a just to be a good person, but to be God's person.

This is what we are freed to be.

But true freedom has to deal with the reality of what we need to be freed from first. It has to take account of a huge issue, one that Paul addresses in Romans. A massive freedom-killer is this: that not all of your appetites are good. In fact, if you are honest, you can quickly find yourself struggling with some of them. It's what Scripture call, 'the law of sin.' Our habit of stuffing things up a bit.

During the fourteenth century Raynald III, was a duke in what is now Belgium. As the result of a violent quarrel, Raynald's younger brother Edward successfully revolted against him. When Edward captured Raynald he built a room around him featuring windows and a door and promised him that the day he left the room his title and property would be returned to him. The problem with this arrangement was that Raynald was grossly overweight and could not fit through the openings in the room. Raynald needed to lose weight before he could leave the room. Edward knew that his older brother could not control his appetite and sent him delicious food every day. As you may imagine, Raynald grew fatter during this time.

Anytime someone accused Duke Edward of treating Raynald cruelly he said: 'My brother is not a prisoner. He may leave when he so wills.'

Raynald stayed in that room for ten years and wasn't released until after Edward died in battle. By then his health was so ruined he died within a year. He was a prisoner of his own appetite.

Just as Raynald was enslaved by his appetite, sin will enslave all those who yield to it.

In Romans 8 Paul is addressing freedom blockers, and he's about to unpack the key to freedom. What we are about to hear is deep, multifaceted, and the most liberating truth in the universe. There's lots to it, because there are many ways we need to be free, and God is of infinite wisdom.

But if we can grasp this deep in our souls we will sing like a bird, flying on the wings of grace.

The first freedom blocker is that we have an inner compulsion to sin. Not all of our attitudes, desires, or appetites lead us to good places. We can't help it. Paul says we need to be delivered, 'from the law of sin and death'. I can be pretty sure everyone in here is included in that. Do I really need to lift the lid off your soul, or mine, to show that our ability to live freely, lightly and joyfully is somewhat blighted by the ease at which we can be negative or hurtful about others, ourselves, the world or God?

Yet the thing is, we are God's image bearers and we want the good. Nearly everyone, believer or not, has an impulse to yearn for the good in the world, and in themselves. But again and again we find that we can't in ourselves respond fully to God's moral imperative or His norms. We find ourselves in this conundrum: we might want to do God's will. Paul says, 'in my mind am a slave to God's law...' I love it. I see the sense in it, the freedom in it brings. But the catch is, 'in my sinful nature a slave to the law of sin.' We can't do it by ourselves. Secularised wisdom acknowledges this. Sheer human effort is not enough to reflect divine holiness. That's why the road to hell is paved with good intentions. We are very good at knowing what is right. Following through is another thing. Anyone who has tried to beat an addiction will know that the first two steps are 'We admitted we were powerless over alcohol' and only a power greater than ourselves could save us.'

We are born for freedom. But our capacity to fall short of what we long for, to not submit to what God requires, and our existence in a world governed by death and spiritual forces which can drag us from God, and from who we are made to be.

To echo Paul, we find this law at work: Although we want to do good, evil is right there with us. For in our inner beings we delight in God's law; but we see another law at work in us, waging war against the law of our minds and making us prisoners of the law of sin at work within us. We want to escape our cell, but our own selves keep stopping us getting through the door.

We are less free than we think. We are not made for this. We are made to experience inner freedom and joy, whatever we have done, whatever we continue to do.

Who will bring us freedom? Who will deliver us? And how?

So much religion is about trying to do the right thing to earn God's favour, His love, His approval. As we have said before, this leads to anxiety, miserable people and even miserable Christians.

I say this because I know what it's like to be a miserable Christian, profoundly aware of my compulsion to sin, and my inability to do nothing about it, but still living like Raynald in his cell. To not be living in cross shaped freedom and joy, but not to feel like the lost sheep carried home, over which the angels party, but the elder brother, filled with resentment, burnout, stress and misery. The opposite of freedom! Some days that still seeps through.

On those days could you say to me, and could we say to each other,

'Guy, trust that God has done it. The power of sin has been broken. Hear these words of grace: there is now no condemnation for those in Christ Jesus. None. Ever. You will muck things up today. No condemnation. You will forget God tomorrow. No condemnation. You will let yourself down and God down next week. No condemnation.'

And I protest, 'Shouldn't I do something about this? That sounds ridiculous.'

And you reply, 'No JESUS saves. Not you. That's the meaning of his name...' And Paul joins in, 'Live in the freedom of a cross-shaped life. Everything you are is identified only with what Jesus has done for you. God hasn't dealt with the problem as something remote and unimportant. In his Son, Jesus, he personally took on the human condition, entered the disordered mess of struggling humanity in order to set it right once and for all....' The road of doing it on your own is a dead end...you will constantly be obsessed with measuring your own moral muscle but never get around to exercising it in real life.'

The power of sin and darkness has been broken, once and for all. Surrendering to this as the cross-shape of your life is the doorway to being able to surrender to God's Spirit – the only Spirit who can change us – and knowing God intimately as a Father.

For Paul this unlocks some ground-shifting truths that pierce our soul and shape our lives:

Do you know that the Spirit who comes to live in you has the same power that raised Jesus from the dead?
Do you know that God wants to be your Abba Father forever?
Do you know that your life is not about believing in God or knowing about God, but loving God who wants you to enjoy the glorious freedom of the children of God?

I suspect many of us have heard this stuff before, in one form or other. But I was slightly disturbed by hearing recently of a Catholic nun who was doing some research and sent a question to a number of people, including, priests, asking, 'What is your lived experience of God?' It was a question that caused some hesitation. More than quite a few found it hard to answer.

God wants you to know inner freedom and joy! That's why He went for the jugular. To set you free! But what does that look like in your lived experience?

For sure, one sermon isn't going to do it. So I have an epiphany gift for you. It's seven meditations from Romans 8, for each day of this week, that are about grasping hold of the freedom of no condemnation in your lived experience. And they all spell together: freedom! I recommend you use them with others if you can – prayer partners, communities, friends, WhatsApp groups.

Grace is your song. The song that sets you free. There's a prayer in an old book called 'Prayers of Life' by Catholic priest Michel Quoist that I used to go to when I was being a miserable Christian. It's called 'Sin' and begins with a familiar lament. 'I have fallen, Lord, once more. I can't go on, I'll never succeed...' The prayer concludes with God replying with these words, 'Come on, son, look up. Isn't it mainly your vanity that is wounded? If you loved me, you would grieve, but you would trust. Do you think there's a limit to God's love? Do you think that for a moment I stopped loving you? But you still rely on yourself, son. You must rely only on me.. Ask my pardon And get up quickly. You see, it's not falling that is the worst, but staying on the ground.'

You have been crucified with Christ and your life is cross-shaped. May you above all live in the freedom and joy that that brings. No more condemnation. No more moral muscle...Free to love God, love yourself, in deep, eternal, real, inner freedom. To live a cross-shaped life for his glory, whose service is perfect freedom!

St Mark's

A journey into freedom
in Romans 8: 1-17,
with a meditation for seven days.

Fully dealt with…"Therefore, there is now no condemnation for those who are in Christ Jesus…God went for the jugular when he sent his own Son. He didn't deal with the problem as something remote and unimportant. In his Son, Jesus, he personally took on the human condition, entered the disordered mess of struggling humanity in order to set it right once and for all."

How are you embracing the complete forgiveness Jesus offers you?

Realistic about yourself. …"The mind governed by the flesh is hostile to God; it does not submit to God's law, nor can it do so. Those who are in the realm of the flesh cannot please God."

Are you able to be realistic about yourself?
How might you still be trying to earn God's love through your behaviour?

Eyes on God. …"…those who live in accordance with the Spirit have their minds set on what the Spirit desires. The mind governed by the flesh is death, but the mind governed by the Spirit is life and peace….Those who trust God's action in them find that God's Spirit is in them—living and breathing God! Obsession with self in these matters is a dead end; attention to God leads us out into the open, into a spacious, free life. Focusing on the self is the opposite of focusing on God."

How can you take your eyes off yourself and fix them on God today?

Embrace your identity…"The Spirit you received does not make you slaves, so that you live in fear again; rather, the Spirit you received brought about your adoption to sonship. And by him we cry, "Abba, Father." …God's Spirit touches our spirits and confirms who we really are. We know who he is, and we know who we are: Father and children. And we know we are going to get what's coming to us—an unbelievable inheritance!"

How can you rejoice in your identity in your lived experience?

Dependent on the Spirit. …"And now what the law code asked for but we couldn't deliver is accomplished as we, instead of redoubling our own efforts, simply embrace what the Spirit is doing in us….It stands to reason, doesn't it, that if the alive-and-present God who raised Jesus from the dead moves into your life, he'll do the same thing in you that he did in Jesus, bringing you alive to himself? When God lives and breathes in you (and he does, as surely as he did in Jesus), you are delivered from that dead life. With his Spirit living in you, your body will be as alive as Christ's!"

How can you stop trying too hard, and start depending on God's Spirit in you?

Open to the Future…"So don't you see that we don't owe this old do-it-yourself life one red cent. There's nothing in it for us, nothing at all. The best thing to do is give it a decent burial and get on with your new life. God's Spirit beckons. There are things to do and places to go!…This resurrection life you received from God is not a timid, grave-tending life. It's adventurously expectant, greeting God with a childlike "What's next, Papa?""

How does God want you to live freely today?

Motivated by Love…."The Spirit you received does not make you slaves, so that you live in fear again; rather, the Spirit you received brought about your adoption to sonship."

How can you serve God out of love, rather than fear, today?

JESUS' FAMILY OF SERVANTS ON MISSION
FOLLOW CHRIST · SHARE JESUS · BE FAMILY | TRANSFORM COMMUNITIES

The ABC of God Confidence

Romans 8:28-39
Wayne Brown. 13th January 2019

In Romans 8:31 we hear the phrase 'If God is for us, who can be against us?' But if that is the case why are so many of us lacking in confidence? Why are so many Christians failing to take the freedom that God has given us and walk in confidence? If we live a life shaped on the cross then our lives ought to be lived out with supreme God-confidence.

When I was a teenager a local cricket team had an open trial. Now I wasn't keen on going but my friends persuaded me to go along, and – shall we say it politely – I didn't have a good day. But worse of all the coach made a withering remark about me in front of the whole trial of about 50 boys, most of whom went to the same school as me. My confidence with cricket bat and ball disappeared immediately. A few weeks later about 6-8 of my friends were knocking at my door trying to get me to play that night as they couldn't get 11 people together to make a team. They were begging me. They were telling me I couldn't let my friends down and that I had to play. Do you know what I did? I said no. My confidence was so far gone, so shot, that I was willing to take the contempt of my friends rather than to try play the game.

What Is Confidence?

Confidence is not reality. It's what you think about reality. What something *is* and how you feel about are very different things. Confidence is ultimately our aptitude to engage with the world. A confident person is able to rise to new challenges, take control of difficult situations, act on opportunities, and accept responsibility and criticism if things go wrong.

I'm not suggesting that everyone has to become an extrovert. You can be a confident introvert. And I'm certainly cognisant that for many of us with low confidence it is deep-seated and long-held. What I am talking about is being a person who eagerly embraces the world rather than allowing the world to dictate terms to you.

Hebrews 10:35 says 'Do not throw away your confidence; it will be richly rewarded'. A lack of confidence is debilitating. People with low confidence tend to see the world as a hostile place and themselves as a victim. As a result, they are reluctant to express and assert themselves, miss out on experiences and opportunities, and feel powerless to change things. The life that God wants us to have is so often held back by our lack of confidence.

God Confidence

But as Christians we have absolutely no excuse. If we lack confidence, really what we are lacking in is faith. In Romans 8:39 we hear that, 'nothing can separate us from the love of Christ' but do we really live like we know that? Instead of walking in God-confidence with this as the underpinning of our life, we end up basing our confidence (or lack of) on external things. But for Christians it absolutely shouldn't be this way.

There is a fantastic story in the bible about King Hezekiah, who was a king in ancient Israel. It's told in 3 separate places, 2 Kings, 2 Chronicles, and Isaiah. Israel is under siege and the King of Assyria sent a huge army of 185k soldiers to Jerusalem and they called for King Hezekiah. The field commander said to the Kings' representatives, 'On what are you basing this confidence of yours? On whom are you depending that you rebel against me? Do not let Hezekiah persuade you to trust in the Lord. Make peace with me or choose death.' On hearing the proclamation Hezekiah went to the temple and prayed to God to deliver them and that night thousands of Assyrian soldiers died and they broke camp and withdrew.

A Confidence Based On A Solid Foundation
A non-believer would look at that situation and their confidence would crumble. But Hezekiah's confidence was not based on external things, it was based upon a knowledge that God was real, that God was with him, and that God was for him. It was God-confidence and it was based on something rock solid. In Matthew 7:24-25 Jesus said, 'Therefore everyone who hears these words of mine and puts them into practice is like a wise person who built their house on the rock. The rain came down, the streams rose, and the winds blew and beat against that house; yet it did not fall, because it had its foundation on the rock.'

Action From Confidence
Some years ago there was an entrepreneur who was deep in debt and could see no way out. They were sat on a park bench contemplating if anything could save the company from bankruptcy. A man sat down and said 'I can see that something is troubling you.' After listening to the woes the man said, 'I believe I can help you.' He wrote out a cheque and said 'Take this money. Meet me here exactly one year from today, and you can pay me back at that time.'

The entrepreneur saw that the cheque was for $500,000 and was signed by John D. Rockefeller, then one of the richest men in the world! They decided to put the uncashed cheque in their safe in the hope that it might give them the strength to work out a way to save their business. With renewed optimism, better deals were negotiated and terms of payment were extended. Several big sales were closed and within a few months they were out of debt and making money once again.

Exactly one year later, they returned to the park with the uncashed cheque. At the agreed-upon time, the man appeared. But just as the entrepreneur was about to hand back the cheque and share his success story, a nurse came running up and grabbed the man. 'I hope he hasn't been bothering you' she said, 'He's always running away from us and making up stories about being John D. Rockefeller.'

All year long that entrepreneur had been wheeling and dealing convinced that they had half a million dollars behind them. It wasn't the money that had turned their life around. It was the confidence that they had gained from a rock solid foundation that had given the result.

Your foundation is God's love, and the knowledge that he is with you, and that he is for you. And if you need evidence, look at the cross. Because of what happened on the cross you can live with freedom and walk with confidence today. You can live a transformed life if you want it. And you can claim privileges of being a Christian right now.

The ABC Of God-Confidence In Everyday Life
In your day to day life remember three things A-B-C:

- A - Acceptance – Accept what you can do and stop worrying about what you can't do. If God wanted you to do those other things then you'd have the skills for it or the aptitude to learn them.

- B - Belief – You are loved. You must know, that you know, that you know, that you know! You should never, ever, ever have to say to God, 'Do you love me?' Any trouble that you might be in right now has nothing to do with God's love for you.

- C - Contentment – If you're trying to impress everyone then you are going to be miserable. I'm up here but I'm not trying to impress you. I'm just enjoying talking about God. I hope that it's good enough but if it's not you'll have to take it up with God because I can't go beyond it.

The ABC Of God-Confidence In A Difficult Situation

So in your daily life, A-B-C – Acceptance, Belief and Contentment. But what if you are faced with a situation where you become faint-hearted? Well, first of all, if you're waiting for the feeling of fear to go away then you're going to be waiting a long time. Courage is taking action when you feel afraid. Doing what you know you should do rather than what the flesh is telling you to do. When facing a situation that needs confidence there is another A-B-C to follow:

- A - Angle – How are you looking at this? Is it really important? Will this really affect you in the way you think it will? Proverbs 3:5 says 'Trust in the Lord with all your heart and do not lean on your own understanding.'

- B – Bible – How does the situation fit with God's word? If the situation or the way you are considering dealing with it is aligned with God's word then don't stress out. James 1:22 says, 'Do not merely listen to the word, and so deceive yourselves. Do what it says.'

- C – Consequences – Are the consequences of failure really as big as you think they are? Proverbs 28:26 says 'The person that trusts in their own heart is a fool!' We talk ourselves into thinking we cannot fail and most of the time it doesn't matter if you try something and happen to be wrong.

A Prayer For God Confidence

Rabindranath Tagore was the first non-European to win the Nobel Prize in Literature. He wasn't a Christian but he perfectly encapsulates how we should feel about God-confidence in this poem:

Let me not pray to be sheltered from dangers but to be fearless in facing them.

Let me not beg for the stilling of my pain but for the heart to conquer it.

Let me not crave in anxious fear to be saved but hope for the patience to win my freedom.

Grant me that I may not be a coward, feeling your mercy in my success alone; but let me find the grasp of your hand in my failure.

Look At The Cross And Be Confident

Jeremiah 17:7 says 'Blessed is the one who trusts in the Lord and whose confidence is in him.'

Every time you look at the cross you should be confident: nothing can separate you from the love of Christ. Paul made it clear: no one can successfully oppose us because God is on our side. No one can successfully make a charge against us because God is judge and jury. And no one can condemn us because Jesus is sat at the right hand of God interceding on our behalf. If no one can oppose us, no one can charge us, and no one can condemn us, then we should have an innate, deeply held sense of confidence that nothing and no one can take away.

Are you a Christian that is alive or are you just breathing? Are you seizing the rights that have been won for you on the cross by our saviour or do you go to church on Sunday and then spend the other 6.5 days of the week just like everyone else? *Real* confidence is only open to believers. It's a privilege of cross-shaped living. It's a genuine, deep seated knowledge that you can walk with your head held high knowing that whatever happens to you, God is on your side. Amen.

Baptised into Christ

Romans 6:1-12
John Duff. 20th January 2019

I want to begin by unveiling the elephant in the room – sin is fun. Much of the time sin is enjoyable. I'm told that if you follow the Slimming World diet (other diets are available) each day you are allowed a certain number of 'sins'. Guess what they are – treats, something enjoyable.

When Satan tempted Jesus he didn't say 'I will give you a life of unending hardship and excruciating pain if you will bow down and worship me' – he offered him fame, honour, power, wealth, importance, influence – all things that could have been attractive. Temptation is only tempting because it is offering us something attractive. Unsurprisingly I have not recently been tempted to put my head in a bucket of freezing water – there is simply no enjoyment for me in that. Let's be honest, when you hear some juicy gossip about someone is it more attractive to keep it to yourself or to share it with someone else?

This is the situation Paul addresses in our Epistle reading. How did he get there? In chapter 1 he has pointed out that while we could in theory all know about God from the world he has created we have chosen not to pursue that and God has let us follow our own pursuit of trying to achieve life through what has been created rather than the creator. In subsequent chapters he has told his readers that despite our best efforts we choose our way not God's way. The Law of Moses, including the Ten Commandments, actually seems to make matters worse, because far from obeying it the end result is that we are more aware when we are tempted and give in to temptation. Like the parishioner who said to the new vicar at the door at the end of a service 'We didn't know what sin was vicar, until you came.'

Paul has also pointed out the serious consequence of sin. If you take a magnet it will have a north pole and a south pole. If you cut the magnet in half you will not have a north magnet and a south magnet – you will have two magnets each with a north and south pole. Paul says sin and death are inseparable like north and south poles. So we are trapped, which Paul summaries in Romans 3:22-23:

'There is no difference between Jew and Gentile, for all have sinned and fall short of the glory of God.'

If you try to jump across a ravine it doesn't matter if you fall short by 30 feet or 3 inches, the inevitable plunge to death is the same. Indeed in chapter 2 Paul warns us not to judge others for that very reason. 'You are a much worse jumper than me, pal' is ridiculous as we both fall together into the ravine.

However we need to read Romans 3:24 too:

'and all are justified freely by his grace through the redemption that came by Jesus Christ.'

If someone reached out and grabbed us to prevent us falling into the ravine we couldn't claim any credit for surviving, but would, I hope, be unendingly grateful to our saviour. Paul calls that faith.

He then introduces us to the second inseparable pairing of the resurrection of Jesus and eternal life which is God's gracious gift to us. Right at the end of chapter 5 Paul explains that where sin was and is plentiful God's grace is even more plentiful.

Back to the elephant: shall we go on sinning because we both enjoy it and because it will demonstrate even more clearly God's grace? Commentators have speculated that this may well have been a serious question that converts were asking Paul and to answer it Paul explains something about our new identity in Christ. In the rest of this chapter and the next Paul effectively says this:

Before you were baptised into Christ it was normal behaviour for you to sin, however now it is abnormal behaviour. The temptation to sin came from your old nature but now anyone who is in Christ is a new creation and the temptation comes from the sin itself.

Paul bases his argument on the reality of which baptism is a sign and symbol. The baptising of converts would have been familiar to his readers and by full immersion: it meant being lowered into the water, consumed by it and then raised up out of the water.

Your new identity is of someone in whom sin and death were inseparable, but as Christ died you also died, and went down into the deep waters of death. The old you sinned and died when Christ died.

Your new identity is the person who was raised with Christ in his resurrection and came up out of the water as a new creation. In you the resurrection of Jesus and eternal life are now inseparable – because he lives you will live, because he has a future you have a future.

There is still a struggle with sin as Paul explains in graphic detail in the rest of this chapter and chapter 7, however we now struggle as those who may lose the odd battle, but have won the war.

Paul explains how to work on this by saying:

'In the same way consider yourself dead to sin but alive to God in Christ Jesus'

The word Paul uses for 'consider' is '*logizesthe*' which is a bookkeeping term. Even though we are still fallible God has made an entry in the eternal books that renders us 'dead to sin, but alive to God.' In eternal reality you are in the 'resurrection/eternal life' column, not the 'sin/death' column and Paul invites his readers to see themselves in that way. To deliberately continue to sin he suggests would be like a prisoner choosing to remain sitting in a cell once the door had been unlocked and they were free to go.

Thinking about being baptised into Christ reminded me of something that happened at my previous church in Lincoln.

There was a time when we were seeing a number of adults come to Christ who had not been baptised as infants. They wanted to be baptised, and we wanted to baptise them, by full immersion. But we were a small Anglican church with a font about the size of the one here.

So the PCC came up with a novel idea – we contacted a local hire company and rented a rubbish skip which they put in our car park. We got the fire brigade to come and fill it with (very cold) water. The hire company was so taken with the idea they cleaned the skip and painted the inside of it blue. We even made the national press as the Anglican Church that baptises people in a rubbish skip.

However what started as a solution to a practical problem became a wonderful illustration of being baptised into Christ. How better to demonstrate that we have died with Christ and left our old nature behind than to leave that, symbolically, in a rubbish skip. To come up out of the water and climb out of the skip to live a new life, with a new identity in Christ.

This reality can help us in times of difficulty, temptation and doubt – it is said of the great reformer Martin Luther, without whose influence St Marks probably wouldn't exist, that he had hours during which he was confused about everything—about the Reformation, about his faith, even about the work of Jesus Christ Himself—hours when he knew of nothing else to help him (and help him it did) save the writing in chalk on his table of the two words: Baptizatus sum!

Which means – 'I am baptised.'

The Life of The Cross

We have this Ministry

2 Corinthians 5:11-21
James Handley. 27th January 2019

In the letters to the Corinthians, Paul is writing to the church in the Greek city of Corinth, which he established during his second missionary journey in Acts 18. We don't have all of the correspondence between Paul and the church in Corinth, so reading the letters we do have is a little bit like listening to part of one side of a telephone conversation – it can be quite frustrating, you only get half the story, and it can be difficult to understand the answer because you haven't heard the question!!

However, we do know that between writing 1 and 2 Corinthians, Paul and the Corinthians seem to have had a major falling out. Paul talks about 'a painful visit' and a 'letter of tears', and by all accounts the Corinthians rejected Paul, his teaching, and his authority as an apostle! Somewhere along the line, they were at least partially reconciled, and 2 Corinthians is written against this backdrop of partial reconciliation. Paul trying to restore friendship, while also defending himself against various claims that had been made against him, and to re-establish his authority and the true Gospel.

Given this context, it's clear that when Paul is writing about reconciliation, about things being made new, about no longer seeing things from a human point of view that these are things which are deeply personal and relevant to him and his relationship with the Corinthians, as well as expressing deeper truths about the nature of God and the work of Jesus. In fact this whole passage is operating on two levels, or in two dimensions, and it's only if we keep both of these in our mind that we can start to get the full picture.

The first dimension is what you might call the 'vertical' dimension, that is to say, between us and God. Our particular passage this morning is fundamentally the gospel itself. The Good News that 'God has reconciled us to himself through Christ' (v 18)

According to the Oxford English Dictionary, reconciliation is 'The action of restoring estranged people or parties to friendship' or 'The action or an act of bringing a thing or things to agreement, concord, or harmony; the fact of being made consistent or compatible.'

Simply put, we were not friends with God, but now – because of Jesus Christ – we can become friends with God. We were living lives at odds with God's perfect and wonderful plan, but now our lives can be reconciled to it.

Paul paints a picture of reconciliation through a series of contrasts. In verse 16, we used to see things from a human point of view, but no longer. In verse 17 the old order has passed away, and we now live in a new creation. And then in verses 18 and 19, we were once estranged from God because of sin, but are now reconciled.

It doesn't stop there though. It isn't just humanity who is reconciled to God, but the whole cosmos. All of creation. Paul talks about God reconciling the world to himself – a theme he repeats in his other letters:
Romans 8:18-21- 'Creation itself will be liberated ... and brought into the glorious freedom of the children of God'.
Ephesians 1:10 - 'Bringing all things in heaven and earth together under Christ'.
Colossians 1:20 - '[Working] through Christ to reconcile to himself all things, whether things on earth or things in heaven'

In other words, through the death and resurrection of Jesus Christ, the whole of creation is being reconciled to God. As we heard a few weeks ago, Paul unpacks this further in Romans; The first Adam (Adam) brought universal discord through disobedience, while the second Adam (Christ) brings universal harmony through obedience.

This is the Good News! God is reconciling us, and indeed all of creation to Himself, through Jesus Christ.

But of course, news is only news if it is told. Good news is only good news if someone actually hears it or experiences it – which brings us to the second dimension; the 'horizontal'. Paul is not only talking about reconciliation with God, but with one another. In fact Paul goes further than this, and says that we, as followers of Jesus, are the *agents* of this reconciliation. So in verses 18 and 19 he writes that '[God] has given us the ministry of reconciliation ... entrusting the message of reconciliation to us' and then in verse 20 that 'we are ambassadors for Christ, since God is making his appeal through us.'

We have this amazing message – of reconciliation with God – but it is a message that must be shared. We have a message AND a ministry. Both combine to make us ambassadors of Christ – God's mouthpiece - as we persuade, entreat, plea, beg those around us to be reconciled to God, to use the language of verse 20. The message is not only told, it is *lived*. Being ministers of reconciliation is as much in the horizontal as the vertical. Not only do we seek reconciliation between people and God, but between people and people. Just as the vertical reconciliation is a sort of return to the Garden of Eden in the sense of unimpaired relationship with God, so the horizontal reconciliation is a return in the sense of unimpaired relationship with one another, and all of creation. We have a message to tell out *and* to live out.

You see, the message and the messenger cannot be separated. Paul was saying that the Corinthians could not reject him without also rejecting the gospel he proclaims, because he is Christ's ambassador or representative. But it also applies the other way, we cannot have the message without the ministry. We are only truly reconciled with God if we are reconciling with one another and drawing others into reconciliation with God. I'm not suggesting this reconciliation is conditional or dependent on us – but I am saying that you can't have one without the other. The message must be lived.

This reconciliation is both objective and subjective. It is both something God has achieved objectively through Christ on the cross *and* is applied subjectively to you and to me as individuals. It is both cosmic *and* personal. It is vertical *and* horizontal. It is a message *and* a ministry.

When we hear and accept this message, we receive a taste of God's future work in our lives, and in the universe as a whole - our vertical reconciliation. We also begin to model and experience the kind of peaceful relationships in every area of life which are in the time to come, the eschaton – our horizontal reconciliation.

Living a cross shaped life means living in both the vertical and the horizontal. As we know peace with God in the vertical, so we increasingly live not only in peace with one other, but spreading this peace as Christ's ambassadors in the horizontal.

The Life of The Cross

Where true Strength comes from

Hebrews 12:1-13
Guy Donegan-Cross. 3rd February 2019

N.B. This sermon preached on John and Maureen Hammerton's 60th wedding anniversary

I wonder who your favourite Doctor Who is. Like most people I think mine is David Tennant. I used to watch it back then. But there was one scene that particularly wound me up. In this scene you've got people on a planet going nowhere, stuck in their cars, in a dead-end life. They are controlled by powerful unseen forces. And these forces effectively keep them anaesthetised with a bit of religion. 'I will cling to the old rugged Cross' they sing, and somehow it distracts them from the reality of their condition. It's the opium of the people as Karl Marx said. Sometimes I get people who look at me with pity for being a Christian - they think it's a crutch, a way out of reality. A way of keeping myself comforted. Maybe you know people like that.

The truth is I think it's the other way round. The more you follow Christ, the one who embraced life with guts, blood, sweat and tears, and the more you open yourself up to God who is love and created all things, the more likely you are to be awake, to be sharpened.

I don't know about you, but even as a Christian I have good days and bad days. On the bad days I become particularly aware of the sin that can easily entangle me - I'm not anaesthetised about it - I'm aware of it. Sometimes I do feel weary at heart because the battle of loving, seeking truth, justice, and peace can get me down. Sometimes I endure opposition, just as Jesus did. We are in a battle after all. And sometimes I'm aware that the troubles of life are changing and shaping me-and on my best days I receive that as a good thing. I want to be disciplined and that I want to be the person God has made me to be. I don't just want to stay as I am. So if you put Jesus at the centre my experience is rather than denying the problems of life you're more likely to become aware of them. I don't think the writers of Doctor Who have a clue about Christ.

For example, John and Maureen, I wonder how you have found marriage. I wonder if it's always been a bed of roses? I wonder if you've had to run with perseverance sometimes? I expect so. Because the truth is that the more we open ourselves up to the path of love, the more we become aware of how much there is in us that needs to change. Being committed to people, loving them, loving God, can really sharpen you up.

Maybe that image of people sitting in cars, not knowing where they've come from, not knowing where they're going, is quite a good metaphor for how people can experience life. But the biggest temptation when life gets tough is this: to turn inwards. To turn in on myself. To make life about me getting through.

I don't know what the world offers, but I know how Jesus dealt with this reality. And it wasn't by turning inward, by forgetting about the world, by not engaging. It was the entire opposite.

Whatever you're facing, however your feeling, this letter says, 'Fix your eyes on him.' That is the true source of strength. Not turning inward. Attending to him. He is called the pioneer-the first one, the one who leads the way in dealing with this stuff-and the perfecter-the one who did it the best.

So what do we learn about how Jesus dealt with struggles? Well the first thing is that he was the last person to turn inward on himself. In fact can you think of anyone who had more hope of heaven but simultaneously was more engaged with the reality of struggle in the world? Yes he knew where he was going-but that didn't mean that he was anaesthetised to suffering-it meant that he got stuck in. He healed. He persevered. He forgave. It was precisely because of his hope that he was motivated to do this. His motivation was to bring heaven to earth, to enter into pain, to see healing.

And I see this in what John and Maureen have been doing with their anniversary. They could have so easily made it about themselves. But instead, because of the hope, because they believe God is making the world new, they took the opportunity to be a blessing to the community. They put on a concert, at some stress to themselves, to raise money for those in need, to build community, to affirm are young people. They are not people who are turning inward because of their hope. It's their hope that motivates them.

The second thing Jesus did was he focused on the big picture, on His eternal self, rather than on just getting through this life. He wasn't so much concerned with the significance of this earthly pilgrimage, which can so easily be shattered by circumstances beyond your control, but for the joy that was set before him he endured the cross. He knew there was a bigger picture, an eternity to prepare for. Sometimes our ambitions can be so shallow, so pointless.

There once was a rich man who was near death. He was very grieved because he had worked so hard for his money and he wanted to be able to take it with him to heaven. So he began to pray that he might be able to take some of his wealth with him. An angel hears his plea and appears to him.
'Sorry, but you can't take your wealth with you.'

The man implores the angel to speak to God to see if He might bend the rules. The man continues to pray that his wealth could follow him. The angel reappears and informs the man that God has decided to allow him to take one suitcase with him.

Overjoyed, the man gathers his largest suitcase and fills it with pure gold bars and places it beside his bed. Soon afterward the man dies and shows up at the Gates of Heaven to greet St. Peter. St. Peter seeing the suitcase says,
'Hold on, you can't bring that in here!'

But, the man explains to St. Peter that he has permission and asks him to verify his story with the Lord. Sure enough, St. Peter checks and comes back saying,
'You're right. You are allowed one carry-on bag, but I'm supposed to check its contents before letting it through.'

St. Peter opens the suitcase to inspect the worldly items that the man found too precious to leave behind and exclaims,
'You brought pavement?!?!?'

Jesus told us to store our treasure in heaven. In other words, not live as if our significance, achievements or success now is the be all and end all. Our characters are being shaped to fit us to rule and reign with him forever. And one day in the new creation will overpay you for 100 years of suffering, challenge and difficulty now. Your future hope is motivation to receive the training that God gives you today.

There is also a theme of reward in the Bible. God notices your struggles, your victories, your faithfulness. One day you will receive a crown. And the beautiful thing is that your heart will be in a place where you won't need to compare yourself with anyone else-have I got a bigger crown? Have I got a smaller crown? You will genuinely be able to rejoice in others' successes just as the evidence of our father's generosity.

And here's something to motivate us to engage. Jesus, we read, endured the shame of the cross for the joy that was set before him. What was that joy? The joy was you. And I. We are his prize. We are what he thought the opposition, the pain, the cross, the torture, the humiliation, was worth pressing forward for. As he hung on the cross your name and my name and the names of all God's children hung on his lips.

If we really see the beauty of our hope, the cloud of witnesses surrounding us, the sacrifice of Jesus, the last thing this will do will be to anaesthetise us, to turn us inward. It's the biggest motivation to imitate Jesus.

So here are three issues that you might want to respond to today, that might prompt you to receive prayer.

Maybe you feel that you are in danger of turning inward - of making life about yourself.

Or perhaps you feel it's time to focus on the eternal work God is doing in you, rather than on small ambitions. Maybe your dreams are not big enough.

And finally, if you are in the battle, Jesus knows all about it. He has endured the cross. And know this - whether you have good days or bad days, whether you are faithful or not, He is faithful to you. You are his joy and crown, the reward he walked the path of Calvary for.

The Revelation of The Cross

**The Lion and the Lamb
Sovereignty and Sacrifice**

The Lion and the Lamb

Revelation 5:1-7
Guy Donegan-Cross. 24th March 2019

Throughout this last year as we have been looking at the beauty of the cross we've been through the whole Bible. We started at the Old Testament, then looked at the passion of Jesus, looked at the diamond of the cross in the New Testament, and what a cross shaped life might look like. We have nearly finished our survey and we going to publish a book in a few weeks time containing all of that teaching.

We end with two weeks looking right at the end of the Bible., from Revelation. Many people find it a bit of a scary and intimidating book. But what I will hope we will discover is that it contains the most beautiful revelation of who God is, and the most complete description of His character.

Let me start with a question. When people make gods, what do they tend to look like? I think they tend to be a bit in our own image - strong, manly, powerful, scary. Think of the Roman god Zeus. Or the Viking gods like Thor. Any superheroes, or X-men...they all reflect the same kind of power. I wonder what your image of God is? I wonder how you think God exercises His power? In other words, what's really going on behind everything? A few years ago a book came out called 'The Secret'. It claims to reveal the truth about happiness - and it says some interesting things. For example it claims if you think enough about something it will probably come to pass.
Hmmmm...Anyway, the point is 30 million people bought this book. Everybody, it seems, wants to know the secret. That's what John is doing in the book of Revelation - revealing the Secret - revealing what's really going on in the universe. It's not a book

so much about the end of the world - it's more about the reality of the way God and the world is.

So as we look at this we are thinking, 'What's the best way to think about God? What is God's power, and God's wisdom like?'

A bit of background before we get into it. It was written by John on an island called Patmos, where he had been banished by the Roman Emperor, about 50 years after Jesus' resurrection. It was written to 7 churches who were undergoing terrible times, being persecuted by the Romans, and trying to work out how to keep going. You can imagine that many of them were tempted to give up. So John wrote a book designed to tell them that whatever they're going through, something bigger is happening. You could say the message of the book is this - God wins. But right towards the beginning of the book in chapter 5 there is this pivotal passage which is the centre of everything.

A few useful things before we get into it because I want you to play detectives and listen out for some symbols. Firstly this passage is set in God's throne room - you will hear about elders who are there - they represent all people through all time. Listen out for the number seven. Whenever you hear the number seven in the bible it means something is perfect and complete. You will hear horns referred to - horns were a symbol of power. If you were lifting up a horn its holder had the power. You'll hear somebody's right-hand talked about. The right hand is the hand used to give authority to other people. There's talk about a lion - in the Old Testament describe when people talked about the lion they were referring to God's saviour who would come to save them from their enemies. And you hear about a lamb. Earlier on in the bible when people needed to put things right with God they would sacrifice an animal. Sometimes a lamb. God gave Abraham a lamb to sacrifice, saying, "God will provide for himself the lamb for a burnt offering, my son'. Sometimes the people had to offer lambs every day. 'Now this is what you shall offer on the altar: two lambs a year old day by day regularly.

One lamb you shall offer in the morning, and the other lamb you shall offer at twilight.' Why? Because sin was serious and needed sorting. The lamb was the way that their sins were forgiven.

So here we are in God's throne room and in his right hand, which is the place of God's authority God is holding a scroll, which is a book, which has seven seals. In other words here is a book that contains the ultimate truth about who God is, in all its completeness, with all of God's authority. Would you like to know what it says?

This is not just the secret that will make you happy, this scroll contains the secret of all things. And an angel asks, 'Who is worthy to open it?' In other words, is there anyone who has ever lived who has the character, the integrity, the beauty of spirit, to be able to open this scroll?

John said in his dream he wept and wept because there was no one worthy to open the scroll or look inside. But then one of the elders says, 'Don't weep, here is the lion of the tribe of Judah who has triumphed. He is able to open the scroll and reveal what is inside.' The Jewish people longed for the lion who would powerfully defeat all God's enemies, who would be the Messiah, the anointed one, ferocious and victorious. Only he has the power and the character.

But here's where the most unexpected thing happens. The lion, the one who is all powerful, turns out to be a lamb - a lamb that looks like it has been killed. The word is a small lamb, a lamb that has laid down its life. Only this lamb can open the scroll. Only the lamb is worthy. It is a lamb with seven horns – in other words - with perfect power. And seven eyes – in other words - perfect knowledge. Who is this and what does it mean? That the lion is actually a lamb? Once John the Baptist was baptising people and Jesus walked by. 'Look!' said John, 'Here is the Lamb of God.' In another letter the writer says, 'Christ, our Passover lamb, has been sacrificed for us.' Jesus is the Lamb. John says he looks like he has been slain. But he only appears dead because actually, he is alive! He has been resurrected! He still has his wounds of death but he is alive for ever.

Who is the one who holds the secret of all things? Jesus, the lion who is a lamb. This is the character of God revealed - He is as ferocious as a lion. But the only thing we experience is the ferocity of his self giving love. This is God's wisdom. This is God's power. When He fights He doesn't fight like Thor or Zeus or any other made up God we can think of. His only strength is the love of the lamb. In Isaiah we read, 'He was oppressed, and he was afflicted, yet he opened not his mouth; like a lamb that is led to the slaughter, and like a sheep that before its shearers is silent, so he opened not his mouth.' The whole Bible points to this revelation. This is the character of God. This is the secret of the scroll. This is the beauty of the cross. Every week when you are here, you sit under the sign of the lamb who was slain and the lion. Can you see them?

A few centuries ago there were a group of Christians called the Moravians. They were very committed. In fact, John Wesley was once on a ship with them and a storm blew up. They immediately started to pray and worship, and he was so touched by how much trust they had in Jesus that later on he visited one of their churches. There he had a powerful experience of the Holy Spirit which changed his life for ever.
Their motto was, 'Our lamb has conquered; let us follow him.'

What kind of God is God? What is the secret of who He is and how he exercises power? Only through the power of the slain lamb. God doesn't fight back with violence - because He knows ultimately violence will consume itself. Instead He lays down His life again and again. Christ the lamb only overcomes and rules through love. The lamb doesn't need us to shout for him. The only question is, when things get tough, when you are opposed, when you have to make a choice as to whether to love your enemy or not, will you follow the lamb? What kind of power will you live by? How much like the lamb will you look? As we draw to the end of looking at the cross may each of us follow the lamb, to death and beyond.

The Revelation of The Cross

Sovereignty and Sacrifice

Revelation 5:8.14
Dan Watts. 31st March 2019

As we conclude this series on 'the beauty of the cross', we finish our journey in the book of revelation. A book that I suspect is unread and unfamiliar to many of us. My guess is that some of you will have dipped into this book, you might have read short passages about scrolls, lamp-stands, animals with 7 eyes and 7 horns, a rider on a pale horse, seals, trumpets, angels, dragons, beasts, bowls, plagues, rivers of blood the list of weirdness goes on. We think this doesn't make any sense, was the writer hallucinating or on drugs when he wrote this. Well no he wasn't, so what is it all about.

Well to give the book its proper title it is 'The Revelation of Jesus Christ' in a nutshell it is all about Jesus – who he is today and what he accomplished on the cross. To fully see Jesus, we must go beyond the images of Him with the disciples, or Jesus on the cross and see Him for who He is today. No longer just a lamb, but a lion, no longer a servant but the King of kings. That's what the book is all about.

We need to understand that this is written in poetic imagery, prophetic language and pictures, a style of writing that was common at the time. We have to differentiate our logical and literal Western (ancient Greek) method way of thinking with the image-based way of thinking of ancient middle eastern cultures.

For example, take a pencil, a Greek/Western mind is focused on its appearance and would say it is yellow, made of wood, is so many inches long and has a point made of graphite. Whereas a Hebrew/Eastern mind is more drawn to the purpose of the pencil, thereby seeing a pencil they would say it is something I can draw or describe things with. In the Hebrew worldview words, actions and verbs are interconnected and often are not differentiated, such as the word 'sword' being rooted in the word to 'cut.'

We also have to differentiate the two methods of storytelling used between the two cultures. Where a Greek/Western mind uses a steady progression of time, with beginning, middle and end, Hebrew writing on the other hand which is seen throughout the scriptures as a poetic flow, where themes, images, metaphors and moments are repeated over and over. It is crucial to notice images, words and metaphors that are repeated; it is done to draw our attention to what God is saying and to confirm that His words will come to pass.

So, what is this vision in the second half of Revelation chapter 5 all abut? We are seeing the response of heaven and earth, we are seeing the response of all creation, to the solution; to the reality that God's will 'will be done on earth as it is in heaven.' And it is the Lamb, the Messiah, who will carry out this divine mission of ultimate justice. But at the same time, what we find here is a stunning revelation of the Lamb's worthiness. Notice that these verses fully answer the question, 'Why is the Lamb worthy? Why is He alone worthy?'

'Worthy are you to take the scroll and to open its seals, for you were slain, and by your blood you ransomed people for God from every tribe and language and people and nation, [10] and you have made them a kingdom and priests to our God, and they shall reign on the earth.'

The Lamb, Jesus Christ, is worthy...He alone is worthy, because He did what no Davidic king could do before: He was perfectly obedient to God, every second of every day for His entire earthly life. And He continues that way. And because of His perfect obedience, He alone was able to give His life as a ransom, in order to redeem, to reclaim, to rescue people from every region, from every race, from every class, from every corner of the earth.

The cross where the Lamb was slain, the day His blood was shed, that was and is the ultimate victory. He alone has conquered sin and death. And as a perfect man, without sin, God has appointed Him to perfectly judge the sin of all mankind.

But His worthiness is also evident from the worship He receives. Verse 12 contains one of only two seven-fold blessings found in this book: 'Worthy is the Lamb who was slain, to receive power and wealth and wisdom and might and honour and glory and blessing!' The other seven-fold praise is found in verse 12 of chapter 7. But that praise is clearly directed toward God. Two times in this book, John is corrected by angels when he attempts to honour or worship them. Both times he is told 'You must not do that,' and he is directed to 'Worship God'. Creatures do not worship creatures. They worship the Creator. But no one in heaven is corrected when Jesus Christ is praised in the same way God is praised.

Jesus Christ is worthy, He alone is worthy, not only because of His perfect humanity, but also because of His perfect deity. He is both worthy to take the scroll and He is worthy of worship.

So, how will you respond?
I want us to think about how this vision should impact us today; how you see God, yourself, and the world around you. Let me suggest two words that might represent a right response to this scene in chapter 5. The words are 'make' and 'break'.

I see the word 'make' demonstrated in the closing section of chapter 5, where the Lamb's reception of the scroll MAKES all creation, heaven and earth, rise up in worship (verse 10). Was that your response? When you think of Jesus, when you think of Him as the 'Lamb of God', of His loving sacrifice and cleansing, liberating blood...when you think of Him as the 'Lion of the tribe of Judah', when you think of His authority and power, when you think of coming judgment...does it make you worship? Does it drive you to your knees, does it cause you to respond in praise and adoration?

We desperately need to see Jesus for who He is. I believe when we do the only appropriate response is to worship Jesus! And what we see here is that the fullness of our worship of Jesus is directly linked to how well we understand the fullness of His worthiness.

What does this look like? Think of the words and phrases we saw in the final section: 'they fell down' (Revelation 5:8, 14), 'they sang' (Revelation 5:9), they proclaimed 'with a loud voice' (Revelation 5:12). Kneeling, singing, and shouting are all classic expressions of worship. We find them throughout the Bible. But even more important than these expressions are the kind of heart that would lead you to kneel, sing, and shout at the top of your lungs...and all for Jesus. Take time to personally consider that kind of heart. That's the heart of true worship.

The second word that I had in mind, the word 'break' is less obvious here. I saw in verse 4 of chapter 5. John tells us that he began to 'weep loudly' when it appeared there was no one who could bring ultimate justice to the world. Now John must have known that Jesus was coming again. As a young man he heard Jesus talk about His return and about the coming judgement and about the hope of the coming kingdom. But clearly, he believes here that all of that is in jeopardy; that maybe he has misunderstood something.

Whatever the explanation, there is no uncertainty about John's response to this cosmic dilemma: his heart breaks for the fate of a world that evidently will not receive divine correction or comfort. If our response to the reality of Jesus is one of worship, shouldn't our response to a life, to a marriage, to a family, to a community without Jesus, be one of weeping? Does your heart break, like John's, when Christ is conspicuously absent from a needy heart?

Brothers and sisters, these two things must go hand-in-hand in terms of a right response. Our hearts cannot burst with praise for Jesus, but then fail to have His heart for a lost and broken world. Ask God...ask God for a heart full of Jesus and for a heart for those who are desperately empty without Him. We are representatives of the great King who is taking back the territory of hearts and minds one person at a time so that all peoples, tribes and nations can be redeemed and join Him in covenant for all of eternity. Our singing and praise are empty and meaningless if they are not accompanied without the will to submit our lives in obedience to the King. To live his way and join in with his plan to redeem all people.

Please do not walk away from this chapter without a clear sense of the radical uniqueness of Jesus. There is no one like Him. There never has been, nor could there ever be again, any one like Jesus. He is our only hope, because only He has and can make things right. He can do that in you, and He will do that in this sick and struggling universe. But he will do it through you and me. Our worship is a life lived in glorious, sacrificial obedience to the rightful King of this world.